Physical Characteristics of the Sussex Spaniel
(from The Kennel Club breed standard)

Body: Chest deep and well developed; not too round and wide. Back and loin well developed and muscular in both width and depth. The back ribs must be deep. Whole body strong and level with no sign of waistline from withers to hips.

Tail: Set low and never carried above level of back. Lively actioned. Customarily docked to a length of from 13–18 cms (5–7 ins).

Hindquarters: Thighs strongly boned and muscular; hocks large and strong, legs short and strong with good bone. Hindlegs not appearing shorter than forelegs or over angulated.

Colour: Rich golden liver and hair shading to golden at tip; gold predominating.

Size: Ideal height at withers: 38–41 cms (15–16 ins). Weight: approximately 23 kgs (50 lbs).

Feet: Round, well padded, well feathered between toes.

D1639511

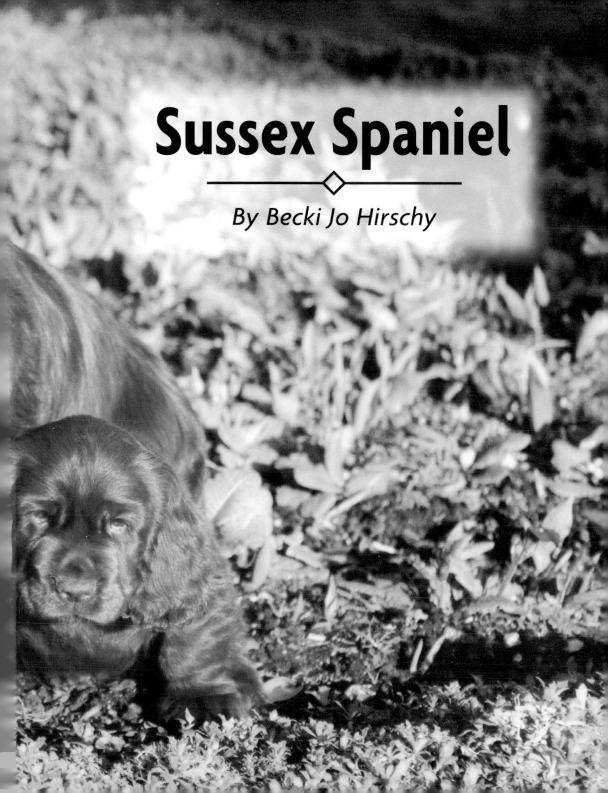

Sussex Spaniel

◇

By Becki Jo Hirschy

Contents

Health Care of Your Sussex Spaniel   97

Discover how to select a proper veterinary surgeon and care for your dog at all stages of life. Topics include vaccinations, skin problems, dealing with external and internal parasites and common medical and behavioural conditions.

Your Veteran Sussex Spaniel   128

Consider the care of your veteran Sussex Spaniel. Recognise the signs of an ageing dog, both behavioural and medical; implement a special care programme with your veterinary surgeon and become comfortable with making the final decisions and arrangements for your veteran Sussex Spaniel.

Showing Your Sussex Spaniel   132

Experience the competitive dog show world in the conformation ring and beyond. Learn about The Kennel Club, the different types of shows and the making up of a champion. Also learn about the FCI, the world's international kennel club.

Behaviour of Your Sussex Spaniel   142

Learn to recognise and handle common behavioural problems in your Sussex Spaniel. Topics discussed include separation anxiety, aggression, barking, chewing, digging, begging, jumping up, etc.

Copyright © 2003
Animalia Books, S.L.
Cover patent pending.
Printed in Korea.

PUBLISHED IN THE UNITED KINGDOM BY:

INTERPET
P U B L I S H I N G

Vincent Lane, Dorking, Surrey RH4 3YX England

ISBN 1-84286-061-5

Photography by Carol Ann Johnson, with additional photographs by:

Norvia Behling, TJ Calhoun, Carolina Biological Supply, Doskocil, Isabelle Francais, James Hayden-Yoav, James R Hayden, RBP, Bill Jonas, Dwight R Kuhn, Dr Dennis Kunkel, Mikki Pet Products, Phototake, Jean Claude Revy, Dr Andrew Spielman and Alice van Kempen.

Illustrations by Patricia Peters.

The publisher wishes to thank Liz Shewell and the rest of the owners of the dogs featured in this book.

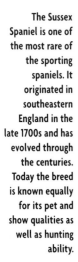

The Sussex Spaniel is one of the most rare of the sporting spaniels. It originated in southeastern England in the late 1700s and has evolved through the centuries. Today the breed is known equally for its pet and show qualities as well as hunting ability.

HISTORY OF THE
SUSSEX SPANIEL

One of the oldest types of dog, the 'Spanyell' was mentioned in literature as early as 1386 and portraits of spaniel-type dogs adorn many Old Master paintings. Although the term 'spaniel' has been used widely as a descriptive term from the 17th century on, since the latter 19th century the spaniel primarily has been considered as an English breed of dog, and so it is with the Sussex Spaniel.

One of the rarest of the sporting spaniels, the Sussex Spaniel originated in southeastern England. Breeding dogs of no particular lineage, denoted in kennel records as 'Bebb to Fan' or 'Old Bebb to Flirt,' resulted in the appearance of the Sussex Spaniel as a more-or-less distinct spaniel type. While it is possible to trace the Sussex Spaniel back well into the late 1700s, it is in the mid-1800s when the breed truly began to evolve and, by this time, the term 'Sussex Spaniel' was descriptive of a specific spaniel strain with recognisable traits.

The Sussex County region gave the breed its name and had

Circa 1620, this scene from *The Vision of St. Hubert* depicts different types of hound- and spaniel-like dogs, some of which are likely the predecessors of today's Gundog breeds. The original painting is housed in the Prado Museum, Madrid.

much to do with the original vision of the breed as a strong and untiring spaniel, fully capable of negotiating the heavy clay soil of the region, which supported thick and somewhat daunting cover. Shorter legs, ability to manoeuvre, a massive body and innate desire rendered the breed ideally suited for hunting this habitat.

Interestingly, this heavy clay soil has a distinctly golden tinge to its coloration, not at all unlike the golden liver colour that is truly an hallmark of the Sussex Spaniel. Perhaps this blending of the dogs with their surroundings resulted in a preference for dogs that used their voices when hunting. After all, when a dog blends into cover, the dog's voice surely alerts the hunter to the

LIVER TO LIVER

In 1872, a rule was enacted that only Sussex of the liver coat colour, who were out of two dogs similarly liver in coat colour, were allowed to be shown. This may well have been an effort of sorts at 'purity' since, despite the lack of modern DNA testing, it was known at that time that breeding liver to liver only begets liver-coloured animals.

location of his dog! Although contested by many modern fanciers, historically the Sussex Spaniel is the sole spaniel purported to 'give tongue'— a rather distinctive sound— when on the hunt.

Mr Augustus Elliot Fuller of Rose Hill is often purported to be the 'father' of the Sussex Spaniel as a breed, according to many accounts. Though the 'Fuller strain from Rose Hill' certainly did contribute to the evolution of the Sussex Spaniel as a distinct breed, it is likely more factual to say that Mr Fuller simply kept and bred his own strain of spaniel for the purpose of shooting over in the Sussex region. Mr Fuller did, however, do much to develop the unique golden liver colour in his Rose Hill strain, with the assistance of his kennel manager, Albert Reif.

With the evolution of the dog show, and later of written standards of perfection for individual breeds, then, as now, fanciers concentrated on producing winners. A rare breed like the Sussex Spaniel was surely attractive for early dog show exhibitors, with its handsome features and solid working ability. After all, in the early days of the dog show, functional abilities were important.

Early fanciers of the Sussex Spaniel in that era were also fanciers of other spaniel breeds. The first Stud Book of The Kennel Club shows that Field, Cocker and Sussex Spaniels were lumped together under one heading. Interbreeding of the three spaniel types was more the rule than the

In the early 20th century, Mrs Youell was considered one of the most important breeders of the Sussex Spaniel. Her kennel prefix, 'Earlswood,' stood for top quality in the breed.

Lovely specimens of their time, Sussex Spaniels Ch Rosehill Rock and Ch Rosehill Rag were bred and owned by Campbell Newington, Esq., of Oakover, Ticehurst, Sussex, and portrayed beautifully in this painting by Lilian Cheviot.

exception, with offspring shown as the variety that they most resembled.

Mr Phineas Bullock is one such fancier and a lead character in the revival of the breed that took place in the 1870s. One of his main studs was a dog named 'Bebb.' Mr Bullock sold this dog, reportedly later regretting that moment of weakness, as Bebb became quite influential in the Sussex Spaniel's development. As merely one illustration of the vast amount of interbreeding between the various spaniel varieties, Bebb's name appears as an ancestor in the extension of pedigree of every Sussex, Field or Cocker Spaniel in the world today.

Though entered in the Stud Book as a Sussex Spaniel of liver colour, written critiques of Bebb indicate that his chief Sussex feature was his coat colour, since descriptions of his features were quite different from those ascribed for the Sussex Spaniel. Again, this merely exemplifies the notion of 'spaniel soup' in the late 1800s. The relative 'purity' of bloodlines

RECOGNITION
Sussex Spaniels were shown in England as early as 1862. This characteristically golden liver dog was also among the first ten breeds recognised by the American Kennel Club in 1894.

INTERBRED REGISTRY
Until 1931, offspring of two varieties of spaniel mated together could be registered and subsequently shown as either variety. After 1931, the interbred spaniel registry came into existence. Thereafter, offspring of the matings of two varieties of spaniel were required to be registered as interbred.

was not so closely protected at that time as in the modern era.

Throughout the late 1800s, the Sussex Spaniel remained rare and numbers were low. Mr Moses Woolland (Bridford) and Mr Campbell Newington (Rose Hill, revived) took a fancy to the Sussex Spaniel. Their kennels established breeding programmes that had far-reaching effects, though probably also contributed further to diminished numbers in the breed. These two kennels monopolised the breed in such a way that it likely had a discouraging effect on others who would endeavour to fancy the breed.

In fits and starts, the Sussex Spaniel tenaciously survived through the end of the First World War, with fanciers coming and going in the breed. At that time, Mr Stevenson Clarke (Broadhurst) took a keen interest in the Sussex for its working qualities, while also having a moderate interest in dog shows. The Broadhurst line

contained significant Field
Spaniel blood, and it is no
surprise that these dogs were
correspondingly longer in leg and
foreface than the ideal. By 1924,
there was sufficient interest to
form the Sussex Spaniel
Association (England) for the
'protection of the Sussex Spaniel.'

Between the World Wars,
other fanciers took up the breed,
notably several women: Miss Reed
(Oakerland), Miss Wigg (Horns-
hill) and Mrs Joy Freer (nee Schole-
field) of the famed Fourclovers
Sussex Spaniel kennel. Photos of
the dogs from these kennels show
more typical Sussex Spaniel
outlines and overall type. Yet,
only the Fourclovers kennel kept
the breed going during the years
of the Second World War, such
that another revival of the breed
became a necessity. Indeed, by the
end of the war, there was a grand
total of eight Sussex Spaniels
remaining, all from Mrs Freer's
Fourclovers kennel. It is
important to note that all modern
Sussex Spaniels owe a debt of
monumental proportions to Mrs
Freer. Without her interest,
dedication and perseverance,
which continued for some 60
years, it is unlikely that the breed
would have survived.

The breed continued to
emerge from near-extinction
slowly through the 1950s, with
years in which difficulty in
breeding resulted in no new

The Field Spaniel's ancestry is closely interwoven with that of the Sussex.

There is documen-
tation of an
important cross
to the English
Springer Spaniel,
a breed that is
popular world-
wide, as
evidenced by this
lovely American-
bred dog.

Crossbreeding to
the Clumber
Spaniel was
undertaken in an
attempt to revive
the Sussex breed
after the Second
World War.

The Cocker Spaniel, another prominent breed in the early 'spaniel soup.'

Sussex Spaniel puppies. In an effort to assist the breed's survival, one officially recorded interbreeding was undertaken to Thornville Snowstorm, a Clumber Spaniel. Three generations of this cross were absorbed into Sussex Spaniel lines. Other crossbreedings, such as that to the Springer Spaniel, Brownie, can be documented through extrapolation. A Sussex Spaniel, Timothy of Oakerland, appears in the Stud Book, having been sired by Sunny South, who, in turn, was out of the Springer, Brownie.

It is important to note these crosses. With the need to inbreed due to the small number of Sussex Spaniels available for breeding, each generation concentrates not only the Sussex Spaniel genes but also those of their ancestors. These documented crosses, along with the 'spaniel soup' from the earliest development of the breed, likely account for the wide variation of type seen, particularly through the 1950s and 1960s, when long legs and untypical heads frequently were produced.

The breed became more settled in type, though still having variation, through the 1970s and 1980s, when a small group of people dedicated to the Sussex Spaniel concentrated on bringing the good specimens forward. Numbers have crept upward slowly such that today the Sussex Spaniel enjoys perhaps the most solid foothold on survival ever.

Today's Sussex Spaniel, looking ahead to a promising future.

CHARACTERISTICS OF THE
SUSSEX SPANIEL

PERSONALITY

A sombre expression, emphasised by a furrowed brow that gives the impression of a somewhat sad frown, belies the calm and steady nature of the Sussex Spaniel. The breed has a distinct personality, and traits cherished by fanciers are the cheerful outlook on life and the extreme loyalty of the Sussex to hearth and home. Showing a distinct preference for his owners, the Sussex may be somewhat aloof, while at the same time polite and gentle, to strangers. Reserve upon first meetings is markedly different from shyness and should not be confused as such. The reserved Sussex will look over the stranger and, upon sensing his owners' acceptance of the new person, will accept the individual into his circle of friends as well.

Fond of communicating their emotions, the Sussex will use his expressive eyes to advantage, while often vocalising with a rather odd snort. It is not unusual for fanciers to refer to the breed as comical; indeed, many Sussex are comedians who develop a plethora of funny little antics that

as much amuse as exasperate their owners. In any gathering of Sussex fanciers, one is at once taken by the stories that abound of the activities of their dogs, who love to be the centre of attention in the household. One comical trait that many Sussex show is a rather gopher-like position in which the dog sits up upon his haunches as if to beg. Another such trait is the tendency of some Sussex to 'grin,' where the dog draws back his lips to expose his teeth.

While a Sussex may be content at times to be a 'couch potato,' do not be fooled—this is a lively breed with plenty of energy to keep up with an active family. An affectionate dog, this powerful spaniel has a strong personality and will seek to be involved in every aspect of his owner's life.

This is a fine breed, and, in the words of Mrs Freer, '...beware, if you become bitten by the Sussex bug, there is no known cure and good sense and reason can quickly go out the window. However, if you want a challenge and wish to work a fine traditional spaniel breed, then perhaps

The sombre, somewhat sad look is typical of the Sussex Spaniel's expression, but contradicts the breed's happy personality.

you should take a second look at the little brown jobs.' It is common for many Sussex owners to describe themselves as being owned by their dogs; this says much about the personality of the breed and their affinity for human companionship.

A PICTURE OF THE SUSSEX SPANIEL

In the initial view, the Sussex Spaniel must be seen as a whole piece to properly appreciate the overall balance of the long, low, level and strong rectangular outline that is part and parcel of the breed. While the term 'massive' is used in modern standards for the breed, the impression of overall size immediately must imply the breed's purpose: to conquer dense undergrowth *en route* to flushing game within gun range of the hunter, who is afoot. Too much mass in comparison to the overall body size, reminiscent of the mass of the Clumber

The distinct golden liver colour, a true hallmark of the breed, is reminiscent of the clay soil of the region in which the Sussex was bred to work.

Spaniel, impedes the breed's stamina and ability to manoeuvre when afield. Too little mass, often seen with relatively longer, lighter-boned legs, implies a speed for work that leads to going around, rather than through, heavy cover.

The Kennel Club specifies height as between 38-41 cms (15-16 ins), with bitches more apt to be on the smaller end of the spectrum. Sufficient bone and muscling contribute to the overall mass such that the Sussex should weigh around 23 kgs (50 lbs); again, bitches are likely to weigh less than dogs and weight will be in proportion to height.

Following the initial impression of the outline of the Sussex Spaniel, one is drawn quickly to the handsome head, with its sombre, serious expression. The impression when perusing the face of the Sussex is that of a frown that is never fierce or foreboding, but rather contemplative and serious. While overall virtue of the animal should never rest solely on the qualities of the head, the head of the Sussex Spaniel contributes as much to the distinctive appearance of the breed as the overall proportion, balance, depth and bone of the body. To emphasise one attribute at the expense of another does the breed no service.

When viewed from the top, the skull is relatively wide yet

rectangular, maintaining a length sufficient to avoid equal proportions of length to width. Without this slightly rectangular shape, the head will appear heavy. Characteristic of the breed, the median furrow (centre indentation) and heavy brow frame large eyes that are gentle, soft and languishing, as if to draw one into the very soul of the dog. The eyes are hazel, in keeping with the gilded liver colour of the coat, and may show a slight amount of haw. Too much looseness to the eye is a liability to the working Sussex, as the dog will be prone to eye irritation at the least from dust, seeds and other irritants inherent in the field environment. With a pronounced stop (the area between mid-brow and muzzle), the face is framed by lobular, large ears, set slightly above the outer corner of the eye and lying close to the skull.

Beneath the eyes, the muzzle is broad and somewhat square when viewed in profile. Ideally somewhat shorter in length and never longer than the topskull, the muzzle is finished with a large nose that is liver in colour, with wide-open nostrils. There is no upward or downward slope to the muzzle and the nasal bone is straight, thereby giving the optimum channel for scenting. The lips are somewhat pendulous. Moderation is the key here, as the dog must be able to pick up game cleanly without interference of the

Size difference in the Sussex is visible, as the bitch (left) is generally shorter and smaller than the dog (right).

flews; it is not a desirable thing for the dog to bite his own lip when retrieving.

Beneath the lips, the bite is ideally scissor, i.e. the upper teeth closely overlapping the lower teeth and set squarely to the jaws. While a scissor bite generally is accepted as being less injurious to game on the retrieve, the bite has less to do with bringing back a bird fit for consumption than does the quality of the mouth. In and of itself, the bite does not denote any tendency toward hard or soft mouth, and deviations from the perfect scissor bite simply are faults.

The head is set onto a well-arched and muscular neck that implies strength. Make no mistake—the proper neck is absolutely necessary to the corresponding proper carriage of the large, strong head, which is rarely held above the level of the back. The head should meet the neck smoothly, without a pointed occiput; any tendency toward a peaked appearance is not typical. In profile, the

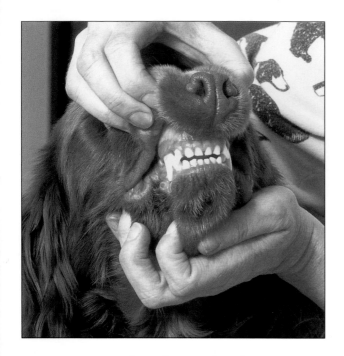

carried low. When gaiting, the tail has a lively action, but never is carried above the level of the back.

Shoulders are set well back and the upper arm corresponds in length to the shoulder blade so that the legs are able to move properly. Forelegs are short, straight and heavily boned, nicely clothed in feathering and set well under the body. Hindquarters must match the bone of the forequarters beneath a strong and well rounded, muscular haunch. The rear hock is short and strong, and turns neither in nor out when viewed from the rear. Both front

While the desirable soft mouth of a hunting spaniel has little to do with the actual bite, the correct bite in the Sussex must be a perfect scissor bite.

neck is clean and without excessive skin.

When viewed from the side, the topline of the Sussex is level and firm with a deep, well-developed chest. It must be emphasised that proper length of rib contributes to the level topline; dogs without sufficient length of rib cage will not be able to hold a proper topline, as there is no supporting structure. The rib blends into a well-developed, short and strong loin that has no appearance of a waist.

The tail is typically docked so that it is 13 to 18 cms (5 to 7 ins) in length for a mature animal. The tail is merely an extension of the spine and, as such, is set and

WEB SITES FOR SUSSEX SPANIEL INFORMATION

www.sussexspaniels.org.uk
The Sussex Spaniel Association (United Kingdom).

www.sussexspaniel.org
The Sussex Spaniel community web site, this is self-described as the 'unofficial' web site for the Sussex Spaniel. Much useful information to help you decide if this is the right breed for you.

www.akc.org
American Kennel Club web site, which includes the AKC's Sussex standard, a photograph and quick facts on the breed.

DOGS, DOGS, GOOD FOR YOUR HEART!
People usually purchase dogs for companionship, but studies show that dogs can help to improve their owners' health and level of activity, as well as lower a human's risk of coronary heart disease. Without even realising it, when a person puts time into exercising, grooming and feeding a dog, he also puts more time into his own personal health care. Dog owners establish more routine schedules for their dogs to follow, which can have positive effects on their own health. Dogs also teach us patience, offer unconditional love and provide the joy of having a furry friend to pet!

and rear feet are large and round in appearance, with short hair between the toes. Good padding of the feet is absolutely necessary for an animal that works dense cover.

When on the move, the Sussex is lively and typically 'rolling' as a result of the relatively short legs coupled with a long and sturdy body. Action of the front and rear legs is coordinated and powerful to propel the dog forward. One should be able easily to imagine the dog's negotiating heavy cover with ease. As such, any paddling, high-stepping or other energy-wasting motions are not typical.

The body coat is abundant and may be either flat or with a slight wave. The neck has a well-marked frill and furnishings appear on the ears, the back of the forelegs, the rear quarters and the tail, although feathering on the rear hock is short. Coat and colour are highly important. A rich golden liver is the only acceptable colour. Any tendency toward a dark liver colour or toward a coarse, thin or 'hound-type' coat is undesirable. The American standard states that a small patch of white on the chest is a minor fault, though white on any other part of the body is a major deviation from the breed standard.

HEALTH CONSIDERATIONS
Fortunately, health problems known in the Sussex Spaniel breed are fewer in number in comparison to many other breeds, particularly in consideration of the narrow genetic base of the Sussex. General good health seems to be a trait with which the breed, overall, is fortunate to be endowed. However, to be forewarned is to be forearmed, so there are some concerns that appear often enough to warrant discussion with breeders. Reputable breeders test their dogs for health problems and do not include affected dogs or carriers in their breeding programmes.

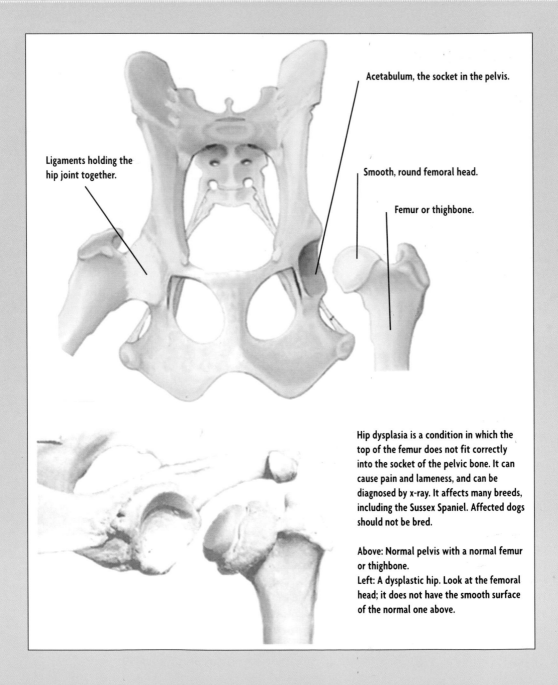

Acetabulum, the socket in the pelvis.

Smooth, round femoral head.

Femur or thighbone.

Ligaments holding the hip joint together.

Hip dysplasia is a condition in which the top of the femur does not fit correctly into the socket of the pelvic bone. It can cause pain and lameness, and can be diagnosed by x-ray. It affects many breeds, including the Sussex Spaniel. Affected dogs should not be bred.

Above: Normal pelvis with a normal femur or thighbone.
Left: A dysplastic hip. Look at the femoral head; it does not have the smooth surface of the normal one above.

HIP DYSPLASIA

Hip dysplasia is an abnormal development of the ball-and-socket apparatus of the hip joint, which is typically progressive with growth and development of the puppy to the adult dog. Symptoms have wide variation, from almost imperceptible to extreme pain and lameness. Virtually every country in which Sussex Spaniels reside has veterinary programmes available to test and rate conformation of dogs' hip joints. While it is not a fail-safe prevention, as factors other than heredity come into play, research data world-wide conclude that breeding two parents that have tested 'normal' for hip conformation tends to produce an higher percentage of puppies with like 'normal' hip conformation.

EYE ABNORMALITIES

Eye problems that can affect the Sussex Spaniel include entropion (eyelids that turn inward), ectropion (eyelids that turn somewhat outward to create a loose eye that shows haw) and cataracts. Many eye abnormalities are considered genetically transferred and testing programmes are available. Again, breeding two parents testing free of eye disease tends to produce an higher percentage of puppies with 'normal' eyes.

Lower entropion, or rolling in of the eyelid, is causing irritation in the left eye of this young dog. Several extra eyelashes, or distichiasis, are present on the upper lid.

HYPOTHYROIDISM

Low levels of thyroid hormones have been well known in the breed for a number of years and are thought by many veterinary researchers to contribute to other auto-immune disorders. While there is some controversy over the heritable nature of the problem, it is safe to say that breeding two parents with 'normal' thyroid function is likely to produce an higher percentage of puppies who will also have 'normal' thyroid function. That being said, hypothyroidism is among the most treatable of any problem, involving annual blood testing and inexpensive daily medication.

CARDIAC ABNORMALITIES

Though puppies with cardiac defects often succumb at birth, some survive for a few years, only to break the hearts of owners with early deaths. It goes without saying that both parents should be cleared of cardiac defects by a vet with expertise in canine cardiology. Puppies should be examined for the presence of cardiac murmur prior to placement in homes.

BREED STANDARD FOR THE
SUSSEX SPANIEL

INTRODUCTION TO THE BREED STANDARD

Breeders and fanciers share the common goal of producing Sussex Spaniels of correct type, handsome enough to win in the show ring yet imbued with innate ability and trainability to work in the field. Indeed, the ideal Sussex Spaniel is a versatile companion, well suited for many activities. It is important to remember the precarious and colourful history of the breed. All of the various dogs used to create the breed in the beginning, and the outcrosses to Springer and Clumber Spaniels in the 1950s, will account for variation in type. One will see Sussex Spaniels who have an hint, and sometimes more, of these ancestors, evidenced by untypical appearance of the head and body. While there have been significant changes to the standard for the breed over the years, it is a severe injustice to the Sussex Spaniel for one to endeavour to breed, show or judge the Sussex without careful study and understanding of the breed standard.

THE KENNEL CLUB STANDARD FOR THE SUSSEX SPANIEL

General Appearance: Massive, strongly built. Active, energetic dog, whose characteristic movement is a decided roll, and unlike that of any other Spaniel.

Characteristics: Natural working ability, gives tongue at work in thick cover.

Temperament: Kindly disposition, aggression highly undesirable.

Head and Skull: Skull wide, showing moderate curve from ear to ear, neither flat nor apple headed, with centre indentation and a pronounced stop. Brows frowning; occiput decided, but not pointed. Nostrils well developed and liver in colour. Well balanced head.

Eyes: Hazel colour, fairly large, not full, but soft expression and not showing much haw.

Ears: Thick, fairly large and

lobular, set moderately low, just above eye level. Lying close to skull.

Mouth: Jaws strong, with a perfect, regular and complete scissor bite, i.e. upper teeth closely overlapping lower teeth and set square to the jaws.

Neck: Long, strong, and slightly arched, not carrying head much above level of back. Slight throatiness, but well marked frill.

Forequarters: Shoulders sloping and free; arms well boned and muscular. Knees large and strong, pasterns short and well boned. Legs rather short and strong.

Body: Chest deep and well developed; not too round and wide. Back and loin well developed and muscular in both width and depth. The back ribs must be deep. Whole body strong and level with no sign of waistline from withers to hips.

Hindquarters: Thighs strongly boned and muscular; hocks large and strong, legs short and strong with good bone. Hindlegs not appearing shorter than forelegs or over angulated.

Feet: Round, well padded, well feathered between toes.

Tail: Set low and never carried

THE IDEAL SPECIMEN

According to The Kennel Club, 'The Breed Standard is the "Blueprint" of the ideal specimen in each breed approved by a governing body, e.g. The Kennel Club, the Fédération Cynologique Internationale (FCI) and the American Kennel Club.

'The Kennel Club writes and revises Breed Standards taking account of the advice of Breed Councils/Clubs. Breed Standards are not changed lightly to avoid "changing the standard to fit the current dogs" and the health and well-being of future dogs is always taken into account when new standards are prepared or existing ones altered.'

Sussex Spaniel dog in profile, showing correct type, balance and substance, and exhibiting the proper coat length and texture for a mature specimen.

above level of back. Lively actioned. Customarily docked to a length of from 13–18 cms (5–7 ins).

Sussex Spaniel head, showing correct type and proportion.

Gait/Movement: True fore and aft with distinctive roll.

Coat: Abundant and flat with no tendency to curl and ample undercoat for weather resistance. Ears covered with soft, wavy hair, but not too profuse. Forequarters and hindquarters moderately well feathered. Tail thickly clothed with hair but not feathered.

Colour: Rich golden liver and hair shading to golden at tip; gold predominating. Dark liver or puce undesirable.

Size: Ideal height at withers: 38–41 cms (15–16 ins). Weight: approximately 23 kgs (50 lbs).

COMPARING SIZE AND PROPORTION OF SOME SPANIELS

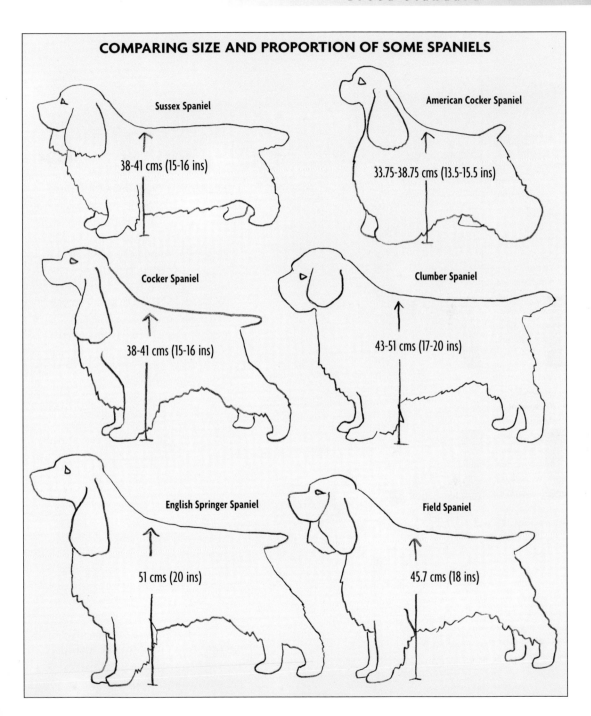

Sussex Spaniel
38-41 cms (15-16 ins)

American Cocker Spaniel
33.75-38.75 cms (13.5-15.5 ins)

Cocker Spaniel
38-41 cms (15-16 ins)

Clumber Spaniel
43-51 cms (17-20 ins)

English Springer Spaniel
51 cms (20 ins)

Field Spaniel
45.7 cms (18 ins)

FAULTS IN PROFILE

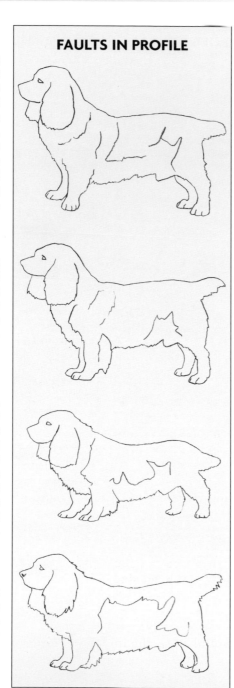

Ewe-necked; upright shoulders; dip in topline behind shoulders; arch over loin; weak, narrow front with toes out; narrow rear, cow-hocked and lacking angulation.

Too high on leg; lacking bone and substance; lacking angulation at both ends, high in rear; flat feet.

Short neck, poorly set onto upright shoulders; weak pasterns; flat feet, too heavy in shoulders, leading into soft topline; steep croup; tail set too low.

Short neck; loaded shoulders; high in rear; lacking proper angulation in rear.

BREEDING CONSIDERATIONS

The decision to breed your dog is one that must be considered carefully and researched thoroughly before moving into action. Some people believe that breeding will make their bitches happier or that it is an easy way to make money. Unfortunately, indiscriminate breeding only worsens the rampant problem of pet overpopulation, as well as putting a considerable dent in your purse. As for the bitch, the entire process from mating through whelping is not an easy one and puts your pet under considerable stress. Last, but not least, consider whether or not you have the means to care for an entire litter of pups. Without a reputation in the field, your attempts to sell the pups may be unsuccessful.

Faults: Any departure from the foregoing points should be considered a fault and the seriousness with which the fault should be regarded should be in exact proportion to its degree.

Note: Male animals should have two apparently normal testicles fully descended into the scrotum.

SUSSEX SPANIEL

HOW TO SELECT A PUPPY

In choosing a Sussex puppy, first and foremost consider your aspirations in acquiring a Sussex Spaniel. Do you wish to show your dog in the conformation ring? Do you want a superb bird dog? Do you want an household companion? Or, do you—as do many who choose the Sussex Spaniel—want a dog that can be all of these while wrapped in a sturdy golden liver wrapper?

While faults, such as legs that are overly long or an head style that varies too far from the standard, may effectively rule out

Bright-eyed and alert, this eight-week-old is ready to go to his new home. Are you ready for a Sussex puppy?

a puppy as a show prospect, faults of this nature are not likely to make a difference for a Sussex Spaniel whose primary occupation will be as an hunting partner or household companion. Most Sussex Spaniel litters have an amount of variation among puppies in terms of type, personality and even size; it is extremely rare that all puppies in any single litter would be show prospects or that all puppies would show the interest in birds that is desirable in an hunting companion.

PUPPY SELECTION

Your selection of a good puppy can be determined by your needs. A show potential or a good pet? It is your choice. Every puppy, however, should be of good temperament. Although show-quality puppies are bred and raised with emphasis on physical conformation, responsible breeders strive for equally good temperament. Do not buy from a breeder who concentrates solely on physical beauty at the expense of personality.

DOCUMENTATION

Two important documents you will get from the breeder are the pup's pedigree and registration certificate. The breeder should register the litter and each pup with The Kennel Club, and it is necessary for you to have the paperwork if you plan on showing or breeding in the future.

Make sure you know the breeder's intentions on which type of registration he will obtain for the pup. There are limited registrations that may prohibit the dog from being shown or bred, or from competing in non-conformation trials such as obedience or agility if the breeder feels that the pup is not of sufficient quality to do so. There is also a type of registration that will permit the dog in non-conformation competition only.

On the reverse side of the registration certificate, the new owner can find the transfer section, which must be signed by the breeder.

Know your goals before you begin contacting breeders; this will be helpful to the breeder in determining if there is an appropriate puppy for you in any particular litter. Speak to as many breeders as possible, in person, by telephone or by e-mail. This is an excellent way to become educated about the breed in general as well as about specific lines of dogs. Questions to ask include:

- How open is the breeder to answering questions from individuals who purchase puppies? You must feel comfortable with the person from whom you purchase your puppy.
- Is the breeder active in showing, hunting or other performance venues? If the breeder does not actively work with his animals in the show ring or performance, what is the reason that the individual is breeding?
- How does the breeder socialise puppies? Are puppies raised in an home or kennel?
- What does the breeder do if your life circumstances change and you can no longer keep your Sussex Spaniel?
- Can the breeder provide you with references of people who have purchased his puppies?

PUPPY APPEARANCE

Your puppy should have a well-fed appearance but not a distended abdomen, which may indicate worms or incorrect feeding, or both. The body should be firm, with a solid feel. The skin of the abdomen should be pale pink and clean, without signs of scratching or rash. Check the hind legs to make certain that dewclaws were removed, if any were present at birth.

- If you are purchasing a Sussex Spaniel as a pet, does the breeder require that the puppy be spayed or neutered? Pet-quality animals should not be used in breeding programmes and a responsible breeder will do all in his power to prevent unwise breeding of dogs from his line.
- Will the breeder provide you with a copy of a standard contract of sale, pictures of the sire and dam and proof of the sire's and dam's health clearances before requiring a deposit? What happens to the deposit if there is not a puppy in the litter that is right for you?

Once you know what your goals are in acquiring a puppy, and have your questions well thought out, the next very important aspect to consider is overall health. After all, you will have this Sussex Spaniel for the next dozen or more years and nothing can break an owner's heart more quickly than a well-loved puppy that is not sound in body or mind. And, much to the dismay of concerned Sussex Spaniel breeders world-wide, even the most cautious breeding of two parents testing normal for all known 'testable' problems may still produce a puppy who will show problems.

Sussex Spaniel breeders and potential owners are lucky in that the breed overall is an healthy

PREPARING FOR PUP

Unfortunately, when a puppy is bought by someone who does not take into consideration the time and attention that dog ownership requires, it is the puppy who suffers when he is either abandoned or placed in a shelter by a frustrated owner. So all of the 'homework' you do in preparation for your pup's arrival will benefit you both. The more informed you are, the more you will know what to expect and the better equipped you will be to handle the ups and downs of raising a puppy. Hopefully, everyone in the household is willing to do his part in raising and caring for the pup. The anticipation of owning a dog often brings a lot of promises from excited family members: 'I will walk him every day,' 'I will feed him,' 'I will house-train him,' etc., but these things take time and effort, and promises can be forgotten easily once the novelty of the new pet has worn off.

one, and that hereditary problems seen in the Sussex are relatively few. Nonetheless, it is important that breeders test their dogs for such problems, and important for prospective owners to enquire about the health of the breeder's line and to see documentation of the sire's and dam's test results. Hip dysplasia, hypothyroidism and eye and heart problems, as previously mentioned, are among the health issues to discuss with the breeder.

It is possible to get a feel for the general health of a breeder's stock by visiting the kennel if at all practical. Realistically, this is not always something that can be done, given the rarity of the breed and the various locations of breeders. For example, show prospects may be imported from one country to another. In some countries, such as the United States, obtaining a Sussex Spaniel puppy may mean not only a long, expectant wait but also the puppy's travelling by air from one coast to the other!

A family portrait of quality, winning Sussex Spaniels. This type of sound breeding is the type of line from which you should obtain your puppy.

'YOU BETTER SHOP AROUND!'
Finding a reputable breeder who sells healthy pups is very important, but make sure that the breeder you choose is not only someone you respect but also someone with whom you feel comfortable. Your breeder will be a resource long after you buy your puppy, and you must be able to call with reasonable questions without being made to feel like a pest! If you don't connect on a personal level, investigate some other breeders before making a final decision.

In these cases, you will need to do most of your investigation by telephone. Ask questions about the health, temperament and ages of parents, and then go on to ask about grandparents and great-grandparents; did these dogs live to older ages or did they die young? What health problems has the breeder encountered in previous litters? Be wary of any breeder who has bred more than a litter or two and who flatly states that he has never produced a dog with any sort of problem!

If you are fortunate enough to be able to visit the breeder, look at and interact with all of dogs on the premises and assess their overall appearance, i.e. are these the type of dogs with which you wish to live? If you are too far

away to make a visit, ask the breeder to send you photos or possibly videos of the parents, the puppies, his other dogs, etc. Reviewing pedigrees can be helpful in some instances. For example, if your goal is a show dog with which to win in the conformation ring, check for depth over several generations of champions in the pedigree. Similarly, if your goal is an hunting companion, look for evidence of proven hunting ability in the pedigree (such as field-trial titles).

If you are able to visit a litter in person, approach the visitation with your head and not your heart. The puppy that is extremely reticent may tug at your heart, but may not be the best prospect if you have a busy household or if you wish to have a dog that virtually shouts 'look at me' to a dog-show judge. On the other hand, this same puppy with a reticent but gentle nature may be the ideal companion in other situations.

Look for obvious signs of health: eyes should be clear without tearing; there should be no obvious structural problems such as lameness; there should be no coughing or raspiness to the breathing; coats should be shiny and healthy, etc. The overall litter simply should have the appearance of health and good nature— physically clean and accustomed to being handled by people.

Finally, inasmuch as you are interviewing the breeder, be prepared to have the breeder interview you! Sussex Spaniel breeders generally are a cautious lot and care deeply about placing each individual puppy in the most suitable home for that puppy. Be prepared for some

ARE YOU A FIT OWNER?

If the breeder from whom you are buying a puppy asks you a lot of personal questions, do not be insulted. Such a breeder wants to be sure that you will be a fit provider for his puppy.

A lovely dam with her promising eight-week-old pup. Be sure to see at least the dam of your chosen pup, either in person or in photos/videos, as she will give you an idea of how your puppy will mature in looks, health and temperament.

in-depth questions about your home, your overall experience with dogs and so forth. Give honest answers, as this will assist the breeder greatly in determining if there is a puppy in the litter that will suit your home and goals. A good match between an individual puppy and owner is essential to an happy dog-owner relationship.

COMMITMENT OF OWNERSHIP

You have chosen the Sussex Spaniel as the breed for you, which means that you have decided which characteristics you want in a dog and what type of dog will best fit into your family and lifestyle. If you have selected a breeder, you have gone a step further—you have done your research and found a responsible, conscientious person who breeds quality Sussex Spaniels and who should be a reliable source of help as you and your puppy adjust to

life together. If you've had the good fortune to observe a litter in action, you have obtained a firsthand look at the dynamics of a puppy 'pack' and, thus, you have learned about each pup's individual personality—you are able to pick out which pups are the leaders, which ones are less outgoing, which ones are confident, which ones are shy, playful, friendly, aggressive, etc. Equally as important, you can recognise what an healthy pup should look and act like. Perhaps you have even found the pup that particularly appeals to you.

All of the background work you do—researching your breed, selecting a responsible breeder and observing as many pups as possible (or making as many enquiries as possible, if you are not able to visit a litter) are all important steps on the way to dog ownership. It may seem like a lot of effort, and you have not even

INHERIT THE MIND

In order to know whether or not a puppy will fit into your lifestyle, you need to assess his personality. A good way to do this is to learn about his parents. Your pup inherits not only his appearance but also his personality and temperament from the sire and dam. If the parents are fearful or overly aggressive, these same traits may likely show up in your puppy.

taken the pup home yet! Remember, though, you cannot be too careful when it comes to deciding on the type of dog you want and finding out about your prospective pup's background. Buying a puppy is not—or *should* not be—just another whimsical purchase. This is one instance in which you actually do get to choose a member of your family!

You may be thinking that buying a puppy should be fun—it should not be so serious and so much work. Keep in mind that your puppy is not a cuddly stuffed toy or decorative lawn ornament; rather, he is a living creature that will become a real member of your family. You will come to realise that, while buying a puppy is a pleasurable and exciting endeavour, it is not something to be taken lightly. Relax...the fun will start when the pup comes home!

Always keep in mind that a puppy is nothing more than a baby in a furry disguise...a baby who is virtually helpless in an human world and who trusts his owner for fulfilment of his basic needs for survival. In addition to food, water and shelter, your pup needs care, protection, guidance and love. If you are not prepared to commit to this, then you are not prepared to own a dog.

'Wait a minute,' you say. 'How hard could this be? All of my neighbours own dogs and they

PUPPY PERSONALITY

When a litter becomes available to you, choosing a pup will not be an easy task! Sound temperament is of utmost importance, but each pup has his own personality and some may be better suited to you than others. A feisty, independent pup will do well in an home with older children and adults, while quiet, shy puppies will thrive in an home with minimal noise and distractions. Your breeder knows the pups best and should be able to guide you in the right direction.

seem to be doing just fine. Why should I have to worry about all of this?' Well, you should not worry about it; in fact, you will probably find that once your Sussex Spaniel pup gets used to his new home, he will fall into his place in the family quite naturally. However, it never hurts to emphasise the commitment of dog ownership. With some time and patience, it is really not too difficult to raise a curious and

YOUR SCHEDULE . . .
If you lead an erratic, unpredictable life, with daily or weekly changes in your work requirements, consider the problems of owning a dog. The new puppy has to be fed regularly, socialised (loved, petted, handled, introduced to other people) and, most importantly, allowed to visit outdoors for toilet training. As the dog gets older, he can become more tolerant of deviations in his feeding and toilet relief routines.

TIME TO GO HOME
Breeders rarely release puppies until they are eight to ten weeks of age. This is an acceptable age for most breeds of dog, excepting toy breeds, which are not released until around 12 weeks, given their petite sizes. If a breeder has a puppy that is 12 weeks of age or older, he is likely well socialised and house-trained. Be sure that he is otherwise healthy before deciding to take him home.

exuberant Sussex Spaniel pup to become a well-adjusted and well-mannered adult dog—a dog that could be your most loyal friend.

PREPARING PUPPY'S PLACE IN YOUR HOME
Researching your breed, finding a breeder and enquiring about the pups and their background are some aspects of the 'homework' you will have to do before taking your Sussex Spaniel puppy home. You will also have to prepare your home and family for the new addition. Much as you would prepare a nursery for a newborn baby, you will need to designate a place in your home that will be the puppy's own. How you prepare your home will depend on how much freedom the dog will be allowed. Whatever you decide, you must ensure that he has a place that he can 'call his own.'

When you bring your new puppy into your home, you are bringing him into what will become his home as well. Obviously, you did not buy a puppy with the intentions of catering to his every whim and allowing him to 'rule the roost,' but in order for a puppy to grow into a stable, well-adjusted dog, he has to feel comfortable in his surroundings. Remember, he is leaving the warmth and security of his mother and littermates, as well as the familiarity of the only place he has ever known, so it is important to make his transition as easy as possible. By preparing a place in your home for the puppy, you are making him feel as welcome as possible in a strange new place. It should not take him long to get used to it, but the sudden shock of being transplanted is somewhat traumatic for a young pup. Imagine how a small child would feel in the same situation—that is how your puppy must be feeling. It is up to you to reassure him and to let him know, 'Little chap, you are going to like it here!'

Your home and garden should be puppy-proofed before you bring your Sussex Spaniel home, as he'll be on the go and ready to explore!

WHAT YOU SHOULD BUY

CRATE

To someone unfamiliar with the use of crates in dog training, it may seem like punishment to shut a dog in a crate, but this is not the case at all. Although all breeders do not advocate crate training, more and more breeders and trainers are recommending crates as preferred tools for show puppies as well as pet puppies.

Crates are not cruel—crates have many humane and highly effective uses in dog care and training. For example, crate

Your Sussex Spaniel will, if properly trained, consider his crate as his private retreat.

PHOTO COURTESY OF DOSKOCIL

their crates overnight. With soft bedding and his favourite toy, a crate becomes a cosy pseudo-den for your dog. Like his ancestors, he too will seek out the comfort and retreat of a den—you just happen to be providing him with something a little more luxurious than what his early ancestors enjoyed.

As far as purchasing a crate, training is a very popular and very successful house-training method. In addition, a crate can keep your dog safe during travel and, perhaps most importantly, a crate provides your dog with a place of his own in your home. It serves as a 'doggie bedroom' of sorts—your Sussex Spaniel can curl up in his crate when he wants to sleep or when he just needs a break. Many dogs sleep in

Your local pet shop will have a wide selection of crates from which you may choose the one most suitable for your Sussex Spaniel.

CRATE-TRAINING TIPS

During crate training, you should partition off the section of the crate in which the pup stays. If he is given too big an area, this will hinder your training efforts. Crate training is based on the fact that a dog does not like to soil his sleeping quarters, so it is ineffective to keep a pup in an area that is so big that he can eliminate in one end and get far enough away from it to sleep. Also, you want to make the crate den-like for the pup. Blankets and a favourite toy will make the crate cosy for the small pup; as he grows, you may want to evict some of his 'room-mates' to make more room. It will take some coaxing at first, but be patient. Given some time to get used to it, your pup will adapt to his new home-within-an-home quite nicely.

Aside from the
myriad benefits
of using a crate in
the home, the
crate is a must for
safe travel.
Show dogs are
transported to
and from shows
in their crates,
and the crates are
used to safely
confine the dogs
as they await
their turn
in the ring.

the type that you buy is up to you.
It will most likely be one of the
two most popular types: wire or
fibreglass. There are advantages
and disadvantages to each type.
For example, a wire crate is more
open, allowing the air to flow
through and affording the dog a
view of what is going on around
him, while a fibreglass crate is
sturdier. Both can double as travel
crates, providing protection for
the dog.

The size of the crate is
another thing to consider. Puppies
do not stay puppies forever—in
fact, sometimes it seems as if they
grow right before your eyes. A
small crate may be fine for a very
young Sussex Spaniel pup, but it
will not do him much good for
long! Unless you have the money
and the inclination to buy a new
crate every time your pup has a
growth spurt, it is better to get one
that will accommodate your dog
both as a pup and at full size. A
size 300 kennel will suit most
Sussex Spaniels. However, if your
Sussex must be crated for any
length of time, such as during the
day when you are at work, a
larger crate will be more comfortable for the dog.

BEDDING
Veterinary bedding in the dog's
crate will help the dog feel more

at home, and you may also like to pop in a small blanket. First, this will take the place of the leaves, twigs, etc., that the pup would use in the wild to make a den; the pup can make his own 'burrow' in the crate. Although your pup is far removed from his den-making ancestors, the denning instinct is still a part of his genetic makeup. Second, until you take your pup home, he has been sleeping amid the warmth of his mother and littermates, and while a blanket is not the same as a warm, breathing body, it still provides heat and something with which to snuggle. You will want to wash your pup's bedding frequently in case he has a toileting 'accident' in his crate, and replace or remove any blanket that becomes ragged and starts to fall apart.

Toys

Toys are a must for dogs of all ages, especially for curious playful pups. Puppies are the 'children' of the dog world, and what child does not love toys? Chew toys provide enjoyment for both dog and owner—your dog will enjoy playing with his favourite toys, while you will enjoy the fact that they distract him from chewing on your expensive shoes and leather sofa. Puppies love to chew; in fact, chewing is a physical need for pups as they are teething, and everything looks appetising! The

TOYS, TOYS, TOYS!

With a big variety of dog toys available, and so many that look like they would be a lot of fun for a dog, be careful in your selection. It is amazing what a set of puppy teeth can do to an innocent-looking toy, so, obviously, safety is a major consideration. Be sure to choose the most durable products that you can find. Hard nylon bones and toys are a safe bet, and many of them are offered in different scents and flavours that will be sure to capture your dog's attention. It is always fun to play a game of catch with your dog, and there are balls and flying discs that are specially made to withstand dog teeth.

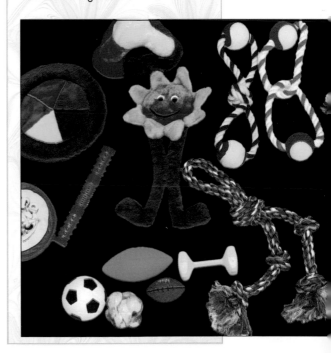

Choose a
lightweight yet
sturdy lead for
your Sussex. If
you choose a
durable lead, it
should last for
years of use.

full range of your possessions—
from old tea towel to Oriental
carpet—are fair game in the eyes
of a teething pup. Puppies are not
all that discerning when it comes
to finding something literally to
'sink their teeth into'—everything
tastes great!

During teething, the need to
chew will escalate as expected
with that developmental phenom-
enon. Sussex Spaniels who are
bored also are known to resort to
chewing to entertain themselves.
It is up to the dog owner to
provide appropriate chew items
for the dog. An appropriate and
generally inexpensive chew item
is a raw beef shank (leg) bone,
available from most butchers, in a
length of 6 to 8 inches. Nylon

bones and other similar sturdy
man-made chew toys are also
appropriate. Rawhide chews,
chew hooves and other similar
items are not advisable. Rawhide
chews quickly become slimy,
sticky messes, whereas chew
hooves may break into sharp
pieces when chewed. Both have
been known to result in digestive
ailments, sometimes requiring
surgical intervention.

Breeders advise owners to
resist stuffed toys, because they
can become de-stuffed in no time.
The overly excited pup may
ingest the stuffing, which is
neither nutritious nor digestible.
Similarly, squeaky toys are quite
popular, but must only be offered
under supervision. Perhaps a
squeaky toy can be used as an aid
in training, but not for free play. If
a pup 'disembowels' one of these,
the small plastic squeaker inside
can be dangerous if swallowed.
Monitor the condition of all your
pup's toys carefully and get rid of
any that have been chewed to the
point of becoming potentially
dangerous.

LEAD

A nylon lead is probably the best
option, as it is the most resistant
to puppy teeth should your pup
take a liking to chewing on his
lead. Of course, this is an habit
that should be nipped in the bud,
but, if your pup likes to chew on
his lead, he has a very slim

CHOOSE AN APPROPRIATE COLLAR

The **BUCKLE COLLAR** is the standard collar used for everyday purposes. Be sure that you adjust the buckle on growing puppies. Check it every day. It can become too tight overnight! These collars can be made of leather or nylon. Attach your dog's identification tags to this collar.

The **CHOKE COLLAR** is designed for training. It is constructed of highly polished steel so that it slides easily through the stainless steel loop. The idea is that the dog controls the pressure around his neck and he will stop pulling if the collar becomes uncomfortable. This collar is *not* recommended for use on the Sussex Spaniel.

The **HALTER** is for a trained dog that has to be restrained to prevent running away, chasing a cat and the like. Considered the most humane of all collars, it is frequently used on smaller dogs on which collars are not comfortable.

Acclimating the pup to wearing a collar is an important basis of safety and training.

chance of being able to chew through the strong nylon. Nylon leads are also lightweight, which is good for a young Sussex Spaniel who is just getting used to the idea of walking on a lead. For everyday walking and safety purposes, the nylon lead is a good choice.

As your pup grows up and gets used to walking on the lead, you may want to purchase a flexible lead. These leads allow you to extend the length to give the dog a broader area to explore or to shorten the length to keep the dog near you. Of course, there are leads designed for training purposes and special harnesses sometimes used with working dogs, but these are not necessary for routine walks.

COLLAR

Your pup should get used to wearing a collar all the time since you will want to attach his ID tags to it; plus, you have to attach the

lead to something! A lightweight nylon collar is a good choice. Make certain that the collar fits snugly enough so that the pup cannot wriggle out of it, but is loose enough so that it will not be uncomfortably tight around the pup's neck. You should be able to fit a finger between the pup's neck and the collar. It may take some time for your pup to get used to wearing the collar, but soon he will not even notice that it is there. Choke collars are made for correcting a dog during training, but Sussex Spaniels do not react well to negative reinforcement; rather, their training should be based on positive, motivational methods with lots of praise.

FOOD AND WATER BOWLS

Your pup will need two bowls, one for food and one for water. You may want two sets of bowls, one for indoors and one for outdoors, depending on where the dog will be fed and where he will be spending time. Stainless steel or sturdy plastic bowls are popular choices. Plastic bowls are more chewable, but dogs tend not to chew on the steel variety, which can be sterilised. It is important to buy sturdy bowls since anything is in danger of being chewed by puppy teeth and you do not want your dog to be constantly chewing apart his bowl (for his safety and for your purse!).

Though no dog owner's favourite chore, you should always clean up after your dog has relieved himself. Fortunately, you can purchase tools to aid in the cleanup task.

Some breeders recommend feeding from elevated bowls, which provide a more natural feeding position. Elevated bowls also are beneficial for puppies, as they make the puppy 'stretch up' and thus prevent him from bearing down on his front pasterns.

CLEANING SUPPLIES

Until a pup is house-trained, you will be doing a lot of cleaning. 'Accidents' will occur, which is acceptable in the beginning stages of toilet training because the puppy does not know any better. All you can do is be prepared to clean up any accidents as soon as they happen. Old rags, towels, newspapers and a safe disinfectant are good to have on hand.

Your local pet shop will have a variety of food and water bowls. Choose durable, easily cleaned bowls; bowl stands also are recommended for the Sussex.

NATURAL TOXINS

Examine your grass and garden landscaping before bringing your puppy home. Many varieties of plants have leaves, stems or flowers that are toxic if ingested, and you can depend on a curious puppy to investigate them. Ask your vet for information on poisonous plants or research them at your library.

BEYOND THE BASICS

The items previously discussed are the bare necessities. You will find out what else you need as you go along—grooming supplies, flea/tick protection, baby gates to partition a room, etc. These things will vary depending on your situation, but it is important that you have everything you need to feed and make your Sussex Spaniel comfortable in his first few days at home.

PUPPY-PROOFING YOUR HOME

Aside from making sure that your Sussex Spaniel will be comfortable in your home, you also have to make sure that your home is safe for your Sussex Spaniel. This means taking precautions that your pup will not get into anything he should not get into and that there is nothing within his reach that may harm him should he sniff it, chew it, inspect it, etc. This probably seems obvious since, while you are primarily concerned with your pup's safety, at the same time you do not want your belongings to be ruined. Breakables should be placed out of reach if your dog is to have full run of the house. If he is to be limited to certain places within the house, keep any potentially dangerous items in the 'off-limits' areas.

An electrical lead can pose a danger should the puppy decide to taste it—and who is going to

PUPPY-PROOFING

Thoroughly puppy-proof your house before bringing your puppy home. Never use cockroach or rodent poisons in any area that will be accessible to the dog. Avoid the use of toilet cleaners. Most dogs are born with 'toilet sonar' and will take a drink if the lid is left open. Also keep the rubbish secured and out of reach.

convince a pup that it would not make a great chew toy? Electrical leads should be fastened tightly against the wall. If your dog is going to spend time in a crate, make sure that there is nothing near his crate that he can reach if he sticks his curious little nose or paws through the openings. Just as you would with a child, keep all household cleaners and chemicals where the pup cannot reach them.

It is also important to make sure that the outside of your home is safe. Of course, your puppy should never be unsupervised, but a pup let loose in the garden will want to run and explore, and he should be granted that freedom. Do not let a fence give you a false sense of security; you would be surprised at how crafty (and persistent) a dog can be in working out how to dig under and squeeze his way through small holes, or to climb over a fence. Sussex Spaniels are notorious problem solvers, and this includes turning their considerable attention to the activity of escaping confinement. While certainly not all Sussex Spaniels work to escape, there are enough stories of Sussex Spaniels' climbing and digging that pet owners must consider the potential.

The remedy is to make the fence well embedded into the ground (about 1 foot deep) and

high enough so that it really is impossible for your dog to get over it. In general, a 4-foot-tall fence is adequate, though a 6-foot-tall fence is preferable. Some Sussex Spaniels who are persistent may require an escape-proof top cover on a kennel run. Check the fence or kennel run periodically to ensure that it is in good shape and make repairs as needed; be sure to secure and repair any gaps or weak spots, and

Provide proper chew toys to avoid your pup's finding something else more to his liking. Sticks are never recommended chew devices, and this pup seems nearly to have uprooted an entire tree!

TOXIC PLANTS

Many plants can be toxic to dogs. If you see your dog carrying a piece of vegetation in his mouth, approach him in a quiet, disinterested manner, avoid eye contact, pet him and gradually remove the plant from his mouth. Alternatively, offer him a treat and maybe he'll drop the plant on his own accord. Be sure no toxic plants are growing in your own garden.

fill in any holes. A very determined pup may return to the same spot to 'work on it' until he is able to get through.

FIRST TRIP TO THE VET

You have selected your puppy, and your home and family are ready. Now all you have to do is collect your Sussex Spaniel from the breeder and the fun begins, right? Well…not so fast. Something else you need to plan is your pup's first trip to the veterinary surgeon. Perhaps the breeder can recommend someone in the area who specialises in spaniel breeds, or maybe you know some other dog owners who can suggest a good vet. Either way, you should have an appointment arranged for your pup before you pick him up.

The pup's first visit will consist of an overall examination to make sure that the pup does not have any problems that are not apparent to you. The veterinary surgeon will also set up a schedule for the pup's vaccinations; the breeder will inform you of which ones the pup has already received and the vet can continue from there.

INTRODUCTION TO THE FAMILY

Everyone in the house will be excited about the puppy's coming home and will want to pet him and play with him, but it is best to make the introduction low-key so as not to overwhelm the puppy. He is apprehensive already. It is the first time he has been separated from his mother and the breeder, and the ride to your home is likely to be the first time he has been in a car. The last thing you want to do is smother him, as this will only frighten him further. This is not to say that human contact is not extremely necessary at this stage, because this is the time when a connection between the pup and his human family is formed. Gentle petting and soothing words should help console him, as well as just putting him down and letting him explore on his own (under your

HOW VACCINES WORK

If you've just bought a puppy, you surely know the importance of having your pup vaccinated, but do you understand how vaccines work? Vaccines contain the same bacteria or viruses that cause the disease you want to prevent, but they have been chemically modified so that they don't cause any harm. Instead, the vaccine causes your dog to produce antibodies that fight the harmful bacteria. Thus, if your dog is exposed to the disease in the future, the antibodies will destroy the viruses or bacteria.

watchful eye, of course).

The pup may approach the family members or may busy himself with exploring for a while. Gradually, each person should spend some time with the pup, one at a time, crouching down to get as close to the pup's level as possible, letting him sniff their hands and petting him gently. He definitely needs human attention and he needs to be touched—this is how to form an immediate bond. Just remember that the pup is experiencing many things for the first time, at the same time. There are new people, new noises, new smells and new things to investigate, so be gentle, be affectionate and be as comforting as you can be.

PUP'S FIRST NIGHT HOME

You have travelled home with your new charge safely in his crate. He's been to the vet for a thorough check-up; he's been weighed, his papers have been examined and perhaps he's even been vaccinated and wormed as well. He's met the whole family, including the excited children and the less-than-happy cat. He's explored his area, his new bed, the garden and anywhere else he's been permitted. He's eaten his first meal at home and relieved himself in the proper place. He's heard lots of new sounds, smelled new friends and seen more of the outside world than ever

before…and that was just the first day! He's worn out and is ready for bed…or so you think!

It's puppy's first night home and you are ready to say 'Good night.' Keep in mind that this is his first night ever to be sleeping alone. His dam and littermates are no longer at paw's length and he's a bit scared, cold and lonely. Be reassuring to your new family member, but this is not the time to spoil him and give in to his inevitable whining.

Puppies whine. They whine to let others know where they are and hopefully to get company out of it. At bedtime, place your pup in his new bed or crate in his designated area and close the crate door. Mercifully, he may fall asleep without a peep. When the inevitable occurs, however, ignore the whining—he is fine. Be strong and keep his interest in mind. Do not allow yourself to feel guilty and visit the pup. He will fall asleep eventually.

Many breeders recommend placing a piece of bedding from

Snuggling with mum is what your new puppy will miss most in his first few nights after leaving the breeder.

the pup's former home in his new bed so that he recognises and is comforted by the scent of his littermates. Others still advise placing an hot water bottle in the bed for warmth. The latter may be a good idea provided the pup doesn't attempt to suckle—he'll get good and wet, and may not fall asleep so fast.

Puppy's first night can be somewhat stressful for both the pup and his new family. Remember that you are setting the tone of night-time at your house. Unless you want to play with your pup every night at 10 p.m., midnight and 2 a.m., don't initiate the habit. Your family will thank you, and so will your pup!

PREVENTING PUPPY PROBLEMS

SOCIALISATION

Now that you have done all of the preparatory work and have helped your pup get accustomed to his new home and family, it is about time for you to have some fun! Socialising your Sussex Spaniel pup gives you the opportunity to show off your new friend, and your pup gets to reap the benefits of being an adorable furry creature that people will want to pet and, in general, think is absolutely precious!

Besides getting to know his new family, your puppy should be exposed to other people, animals and situations. This will help him become well adjusted as he grows up and less prone to being timid or fearful of the new things he will encounter. Of course, he must not come into close contact with dogs you don't know well until his course of injections is fully complete.

Your pup's socialisation began with the breeder, but now it is your responsibility to continue it. The socialisation he receives until the age of 12 weeks is the most critical, as this is the time when he forms his impressions of the outside world. Be especially careful during the eight-to-ten-week-old period, also known as the fear period. The interaction he receives during this time should be gentle and reassuring. Lack of socialisation, and/or negative experiences during the socialisation period, can manifest itself in fear and aggression as the dog grows up. Your puppy needs lots of positive interaction, which of course includes human contact, affection, handling and exposure to other animals.

Once your pup has received his necessary vaccinations, feel free to take him out and about (on his lead, of course). Walk him around the neighbourhood, take him on your daily errands, let people pet him, let him meet other dogs and pets, etc. Puppies do not have to try to make friends; there will be no shortage of people who will want to introduce themselves. Just make sure that you carefully supervise each meeting. If the neighbourhood children want to say hello, for example, that is great—children and pups most often make great companions. However, sometimes an excited child can unintentionally handle a pup too roughly, or an overzealous pup can playfully nip a little too hard. You want to make socialisation experiences positive ones. What a pup learns during this very formative stage will affect his attitude toward future encounters. You want your dog to be comfortable around everyone. A pup that has a bad experience with a child may grow up to be a dog that is shy around or aggressive toward children.

CONSISTENCY IN TRAINING

Dogs, being pack animals, naturally need a leader, or else they try to establish dominance in their packs. When you welcome a dog into your family, the choice of who becomes the leader and who becomes the 'pack' is entirely up to you! Your pup's intuitive quest for dominance, coupled with the fact that it is nearly impossible to look at an adorable Sussex Spaniel pup with his 'puppy-dog' eyes and not cave in, give the pup almost an unfair advantage in getting the upper hand! A pup will definitely test the waters to

see what he can and cannot do. Do not give in to those pleading eyes—stand your ground when it comes to disciplining the pup and make sure that all family members do the same. It will only confuse the pup if Mother tells him to get off the sofa when he is used to

MANNERS MATTER

During the socialisation process, a puppy should meet people, experience different environments and definitely be exposed to other canines. Through playing and interacting with other dogs, your puppy will learn lessons, ranging from controlling the pressure of his jaws by biting his littermates to the inner-workings of the canine pack that he will apply to his human relationships for the rest of his life. That is why removing a puppy from his litter too early (before eight weeks) can be detrimental to the pup's development.

Ankles and trouser legs are at just the right height to satisfy a pup's urge to nip. This behaviour must be consistently discouraged as soon as it begins.

sitting up there with Father to watch the nightly news. Avoid discrepancies by having all members of the household decide on the rules before the pup even comes home...and be consistent in enforcing them! Early training shapes the dog's personality, so you cannot be unclear in what you expect.

COMMON PUPPY PROBLEMS

The best way to prevent puppy problems is to be proactive in stopping an undesirable behaviour as soon as it starts. The old saying 'You can't teach an old dog new tricks' does not neceessarily hold true, but it is true that it is much easier to discourage bad behaviour in a young

developing pup than to wait until the pup's bad behaviour becomes the adult dog's bad habit. There are some problems that are especially prevalent in puppies as they develop.

NIPPING

As puppies start to teethe, they feel the need to sink their teeth into anything available...unfortunately, that usually includes your fingers, arms, hair and toes. You may find this behaviour cute for the first five seconds...until you feel just how sharp those puppy teeth are. Nipping is something you want to discourage immediately and consistently with a firm 'No!' (or whatever number of firm 'Nos' it takes for him to understand that you mean business). Then, replace your finger with an appropriate chew toy. While this behaviour is merely annoying when the dog is young, it can become dangerous as your Sussex Spaniel's adult teeth grow in and his jaws develop, and he

STRESS-FREE

Some experts in canine health advise that stress during a dog's early years of development can compromise and weaken his immune system, and may trigger the potential for a shortened life expectancy. They emphasise the need for happy and stress-free growing-up years.

DIETARY AND FEEDING CONSIDERATIONS

Today the choices of food for your Sussex Spaniel are many and varied. There are simply dozens of brands of food in all sorts of flavours and textures, ranging from puppy diets to those for veterans. There are even hypoallergenic and low-calorie diets available. Because your Sussex Spaniel's food has a bearing on coat, health and temperament, it is essential that the most suitable diet is selected for a Sussex Spaniel of his age. It is fair to say, however, that even experienced owners can be perplexed by the enormous range of foods available. Only understanding what is best for your dog will help you reach an informed decision.

Dog foods are produced in three basic types: dried, semi-moist and tinned. Dried foods are useful for the cost-conscious, for overall they tend to be less expensive than semi-moist or tinned foods. Dried foods also contain the least fat and the most preservatives. In general, tinned foods are made up of 60–70% water, while semi-moist ones often contain so much sugar that they are perhaps the least preferred by owners, even though their dogs seem to like them.

When selecting your dog's diet, three stages of development must be considered: the puppy stage, the adult stage and the veteran stage.

PUPPY STAGE

Puppies instinctively want to suck milk from their dam's teats; a normal puppy will exhibit this behaviour just a few moments following birth. If puppies do not attempt to suckle within the first half-hour or so, the breeder encourages them to do so by placing them on the nipples, having selected ones with plenty of milk. This early milk supply is important in providing the essential colostrum, which protects the puppies during the first eight to ten weeks of their lives.

Although a dam's milk is much better than any milk formula, despite there being some excellent ones available, if the puppies do not feed, the breeder will have to feed them by hand.

EVERYDAY CARE OF YOUR
SUSSEX SPANIEL

DIETARY AND FEEDING CONSIDERATIONS

Today the choices of food for your Sussex Spaniel are many and varied. There are simply dozens of brands of food in all sorts of flavours and textures, ranging from puppy diets to those for veterans. There are even hypoallergenic and low-calorie diets available. Because your Sussex Spaniel's food has a bearing on coat, health and temperament, it is essential that the most suitable diet is selected for a Sussex Spaniel of his age. It is fair to say, however, that even experienced owners can be perplexed by the enormous range of foods available. Only understanding what is best for your dog will help you reach an informed decision.

Dog foods are produced in three basic types: dried, semi-moist and tinned. Dried foods are useful for the cost-conscious, for overall they tend to be less expensive than semi-moist or tinned foods. Dried foods also contain the least fat and the most preservatives. In general, tinned foods are made up of 60–70% water, while semi-moist ones often contain so much sugar that they are perhaps the least preferred by owners, even though their dogs seem to like them.

When selecting your dog's diet, three stages of development must be considered: the puppy stage, the adult stage and the veteran stage.

PUPPY STAGE

Puppies instinctively want to suck milk from their dam's teats; a normal puppy will exhibit this behaviour just a few moments following birth. If puppies do not attempt to suckle within the first half-hour or so, the breeder encourages them to do so by placing them on the nipples, having selected ones with plenty of milk. This early milk supply is important in providing the essential colostrum, which protects the puppies during the first eight to ten weeks of their lives.

Although a dam's milk is much better than any milk formula, despite there being some excellent ones available, if the puppies do not feed, the breeder will have to feed them by hand.

For those with less experience, advice from a veterinary surgeon is important so that not only the right quantity of milk is fed but also that of correct quality, fed at suitably frequent intervals, usually every two hours during the first few days of life.

Puppies should be allowed to nurse from their mothers for about the first six weeks, although, starting around the third or fourth week, the breeder will begin to introduce small portions of suitable solid food. Most breeders like to introduce alternate milk and meat meals initially, building up to weaning time.

By the time the puppies are seven or a maximum of eight weeks old, they should be fully weaned and fed solely on a proprietary food. Selection of the most suitable, good-quality diet at this time is essential, for a puppy's fastest growth rate is during the first year of life. Veterinary surgeons often recommend that puppies be maintained on a food formulated for puppies until one year of age, but this is *not* ideal for Sussex Spaniels. Food formulated specifically for puppies often encourages a rate of growth in body mass (weight) that outpaces the strength of musculature and other soft-tissue support structures. The result is that the front assembly of the dog suffers.

Feed the puppy a good-quality adult dog food. The Sussex

Knowing what and how to feed your new Sussex Spaniel puppy are questions to be answered before the pup comes home. Take advice from the breeder, who is know-ledgeable about what works best with his line of dogs.

companions following the recommendations of any one of several reputable authors to assure that the diet is balanced. Some fanciers also believe strongly in using dog dishes that are raised off the floor. These are thought to be beneficial in providing a more natural feeding position as well as in making the puppy 'stretch-up' and avoid bearing down on the front pasterns. It is always wise to consult the breeder of your puppy about specific feeding practices.

FOOD STORAGE

You must store your dried dog food carefully. Open packages of dog food quickly lose their vitamin value, usually within 90 days of being opened. Mould spores and vermin could also contaminate the food.

Spaniel puppy should be lean. Like the gawky human adolescent, the appearance should portend that there is much more to come as the frame slowly fills out with maturity. The Sussex Spaniel is not a small spaniel by any means and puppies that mature too quickly may not develop the overall size and substance typical for the breed.

Many Sussex Spaniel owners have had considerable success with natural diets for their

FOOD PREFERENCE

Selecting the best dried dog food is difficult. There is no majority consensus among veterinary scientists as to the value of nutrient analyses (protein, fat, fibre, moisture, ash, cholesterol, minerals, etc.). All agree that feeding trials are what matter, but you also have to consider the individual dog. The dog's weight, age and activity level, and what pleases his taste, all must be considered. It is probably best to take the advice of your breeder or veterinary surgeon. Every dog's dietary requirements vary, even during the lifetime of a particular dog.

If your dog is fed a good dried food, it does not require supplements of meat or vegetables. Dogs do appreciate a little variety in their diets, so you may choose to stay with the same brand but vary the flavour. Alternatively, you may wish to add a little flavoured stock to give a difference to the taste.

ADULT DIETS

A dog generally is considered an adult when it has stopped growing. The Sussex Spaniel is a slow-maturing breed, with full maturity often not seen until three years of age. While the one-year-old Sussex Spaniel may have reached his full height, substantial changes can and do occur in body substance, and both in amount and length of coat. Again you should feed the adult Sussex on an high-quality adult food, relying on the breeder or your veterinary surgeon to recommend an acceptable maintenance diet. Major dog-food manufacturers specialise in this type of food, and it is merely necessary for you to select the one best suited to your dog's needs. Active dogs have different requirements from sedate dogs.

VETERAN DIETS

As a dog gets older, his metabolism changes. The older dog usually exercises less, moves more slowly and sleeps more. This change in lifestyle and physiological perform-ance requires a change in diet. Since these changes take place slowly, they might not be recognis-able. What is easily recognisable is weight gain. By continuing to feed your dog an adult-maintenance diet when he is slowing down metaboli-cally, your dog will gain weight. Obesity in an older dog compounds the health problems that already accompany old age.

SUPPLEMENTATION

While excessive supplementation is not recommended, there are some supplements commonly used by Sussex Spaniel fanciers.

Kelp: a supplement to enhance overall immune system function and improve coat, which is used by a number of fanciers.

Vitamin C: this water-soluble vitamin is often used during major growth phases, typically until the puppy reaches two years of age.

Omega Fatty Acid supplements: these oils are often useful, particularly with liver-coloured coats, which tend to be somewhat drier and less glossy than coats of other colours.

Other supplements used vary widely, according to individual prefer-ence of the breeder. It is best to consult with the breeder of your puppy and to follow the feeding instructions given.

Vitamins Recommended for Dogs

Some breeders and vets recommend the supplementation of vitamins to a dog's diet—others do not. Before embarking on a vitamin programme, consult your vet.

Vitamin / Dosage	Food source	Benefits
A / 10,000 IU/week	Eggs, butter, yoghurt, meat	Skin, eyes, hind legs, haircoat
B / Varies	Organs, cottage cheese, sardines	Appetite, fleas, heart, skin and coat
C / 2000 mg+	Fruit, legumes, leafy green vegetables	Healing, arthritis, kidneys
D / Varies	Cod liver, cheese, organs, eggs	Bones, teeth, endocrine system
E / 250 IU daily	Leafy green vegetables, meat, wheat germ oil	Skin, muscles, nerves, healing, digestion
F / Varies	Fish oils, raw meat	Heart, skin, coat, fleas
K / Varies	Naturally in body, not through food	Blood clotting

As your dog gets older, few of his organs function up to par. The kidneys slow down and the intestines become less efficient. These age-related factors are best handled with a change in diet and a change in feeding schedule to give smaller portions that are more easily digested. There is no single best diet for every older dog. While many dogs do well on light or veteran diets, other dogs do better on special premium diets such as lamb and rice.

Sussex Spaniels have a lifespan of approximately 12 years of age (usually ranging between 11 and 15 years of age). The typical age at which a dog is considered a 'veteran' varies greatly. The shift, if any, from adult to veteran dog food should be made based on the needs of the individual animal rather than on age. Veterans often may continue to be fed regular adult dog food with no ill effects. Others, particularly those who are less active or those with weight-control problems, may do better on a veteran food that has fewer calories per cup of dry weight. For veterans with specific medical problems, special diets may be needed as recommended by your vet.

Be sensitive to your veteran Sussex Spaniel's diet, as this will help control other problems that may arise with your old friend.

WATER

Just as your dog needs proper nutrition from his food, water is an essential 'nutrient' as well. Water keeps the dog's body properly hydrated and promotes normal function of the body's systems. During house-training, it is necessary to keep an eye on how much water your Sussex Spaniel is drinking, but once he is reliably trained he should have access to clean fresh water at all times, especially if you feed dried food. Make certain that the dog's water bowl is clean, and change the water often.

EXERCISE

The Sussex Spaniel's exercise needs vary greatly among individuals. Sussex Spaniels from lines bred not only for conformation but also for working ability (hunting, obedience, agility, tracking) will typically need more exercise than those from lines bred primarily for the conformation show ring with less emphasis on performance. On the average, a couple of brisk 15- to 20-minute walks each day, or at least daily sessions of throwing a tennis ball or retrieving a bumper in the garden, are recommended.

DRINK, DRANK, DRUNK— MAKE IT A DOUBLE

In both humans and dogs, as well as other living organisms, water forms the major part of nearly every body tissue. Naturally, we take water for granted, but without it, life as we know it would cease.

For dogs, water is needed to keep their bodies functioning biochemically. Additionally, water is needed to replace the water lost while panting. Unlike humans, who are able to sweat to dissipate heat, dogs must pant to cool down, thereby losing the vital water from their bodies needed to regulate their body temperatures. Humans lose electrolyte-containing products and other body-fluid components through sweating; dogs do not lose anything except water.

Water is essential always, but especially so when the weather is hot or humid or when your dog is exercising or working vigorously.

necessary for the overall health and well-being of the Sussex Spaniel as well as for maintaining a typical appearance. The basic grooming described here is for the

Exercise time is fun for dogs and owner, as it provides all concerned with needed activity and important opportunities for bonding.

Creating a safe place for a Sussex Spaniel puppy to play freely, such as a fenced garden, is helpful to allow the puppy to exercise to the amount that the puppy requires. That being said, all Sussex Spaniels need quality exercise that includes interaction and playtime with their human companions; this is not a breed that will be content to be relegated to the garden without human interaction.

Bear in mind that an overweight dog should never be suddenly over-exercised; instead he should be encouraged to increase exercise slowly. Not only is exercise essential to keep the dog's body fit, it is essential to his mental well-being. A bored dog will find something to do, which often manifests itself in some type of destructive behaviour.

GROOMING
The Sussex Spaniel is very much a 'wash and wear' breed. While grooming for the show ring has considerable variations from country to country, there are basic grooming procedures that are

SUSSEX GROOMING TOOLS
There are variations in methods for trimming and preparing the dog for the show ring among fanciers in different countries. Regardless, the basic grooming equipment needed includes the following:
- Bristle brush (natural bristle-style recommended)
- 'Greyhound'-style comb
- Straight shears
- Stripping knife
- Shampoo formulated for canines
- Tea towel or face flannel
- Hand-held blaster
- Nail clipper and nail file or nail grinder
- Styptic powder or liquid
- Ear cleanser, powder or liquid as recommended by your vet or breeder
- Cotton wipes and cotton wool
- Soft toothbrush and canine toothpaste or other dental-care products as recommended by the vet or breeder
- Thinning shears (optional)
- Grooming spray for daily use (optional)
- Grooming table (optional)
- Coat conditioner for use after bathing (optional)
- SPF-rated sun protection spray for coat (optional)

household companion. There is a bit more to learn for grooming a show dog, and your dog's breeder is often your very best source of information for learning the requirements of show grooming.

BRUSHING AND COMBING

Most Sussex Spaniels absolutely enjoy time with their owners, including time spent being brushed and combed. After all, it is a time when your Sussex has your undivided attention, and regular grooming sessions can be very relaxing for both you and your dog. On at least a weekly basis, use the bristle brush, starting at the top of the skull and working toward the tail, always going with the lay of the hair. Avoid brushing the facial area; use a barely damp face flannel to groom this area, again always going with the lay of the hair.

Sussex Spaniels do shed. Brushing removes dead hair and, with regular brushing, you will see far less shedding in the form of 'fluff balls' of dog hair drifting into corners! A conditioning grooming spray may be used during brushing; this is particularly helpful for dogs that will be shown in the conformation ring, as it helps prevent coat breakage.

Following brushing, use the comb for feathering on the ears, legs and belly area. Gently work out any tangles that might be present to avoid any discomfort to

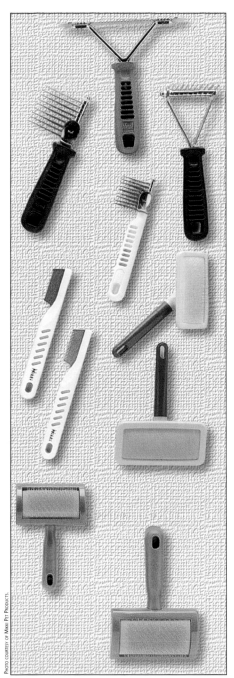

Your local pet shop usually carries a complete line of grooming tools. Follow the suggestions contained herein if you intend to groom your Sussex Spaniel yourself.

PHOTO COURTESY OF MIKKI PET PRODUCTS.

Carefully brush through the body coat. Using a grooming table will make grooming more comfortable for both dog and owner.

A comb-through following brushing will help to remove dead hair and ensure that the coat is mat- and tangle-free.

Don't forget the feathering, such as that on the ears. A comb should be used carefully and gently to detangle these areas.

your dog. If needed, depending on how much time your Sussex Spaniel spends outdoors, a sunscreen spray is helpful to apply as a final mist to prevent bleaching of the coat, which is particularly a problem for the liver coat colour.

TRIMMING
Neatening up the haircoat is helpful in maintaining a typical Sussex Spaniel appearance, whether the dog is an household companion or show dog. Trimming, even for the show ring, should only enhance the natural appearance of the dog. The choice of tools to use for trimming the coat varies considerably among fanciers. It is safe to say that the stripping knife is utilised worldwide to remove dead coat as well as to blend coat or remove excessive length, while the straight shear is used to shorten the hair on the back of the rear leg from hock to ground. The straight shear also should be used carefully to trim hair from the footpads so that the dog is not walking on hair, thereby losing the natural traction supplied by the pads.

In general, the hair on the upper one-third of the outer ear is shortened to enhance the appearance of the set of the ear, allowing the ear to gracefully frame the face. This may be accomplished by use of the stripping knife or thinning shear, both to shorten as necessary and to blend the hair to lay flat and create a gradual transition of the hair from skull to ear to neck. Hair from the lower jaw, an area about two finger breadths above the prosternum of the chest, may also be shortened with a stripping knife to enhance the neckline of the dog. Again, the key is to remove just enough hair to neaten the appearance and blend well into the longer body coat. Excessive facial hair may be carefully stripped by using a small stripping knife created expressly for that purpose.

The stripping knife is the preferred tool to use on the body coat to remove fuzzy hair as commonly seen on liver-coloured dogs. An electric clipper or thinning shear should never be used on the body coat, as doing so will often ruin the proper texture of the coat. As an alternative to the stripping knife, hand plucking of the body coat may be done. Though this is very time-consuming and can take a bit of practice to master, the end result is that the best possible coat texture is truly enhanced.

BATHING

The frequency of bathing will depend greatly on the sort of activities done by the dog as well as on the coat of the individual dog. Some Sussex Spaniels have coats that are oilier than others, and these may become 'doggy' more quickly. Therefore, if your

SOAP IT UP
The use of human soap products like shampoo, bubble bath and hand soap can be damaging to a dog's coat and skin. Human products are too strong; they remove the protective oils coating the dog's hair and skin that make him water-resistant. Use only shampoo made especially for dogs. You may like to use a medicated shampoo, which will help to keep external parasites at bay.

Sussex Spaniel is an household companion and sleeps on your bed, you may wish to freshen your dog up a bit more often! Sussex Spaniels who are shown are often bathed far more frequently, particularly during show season. On the average, an home companion will require bathing no more frequently than once a month, especially if routine coat care via thorough brushing is done.

Brush your Sussex Spaniel thoroughly before wetting his coat. This will get rid of most mats and tangles, which are harder to remove when the coat is wet. Make certain that your dog has a good non-slip surface on which to stand. Before wetting the dog, place cotton wool in the outer ears to prevent water from getting into the ear canals. Using tepid water, just warm to the touch, thoroughly wet the dog, beginning at the head and working toward the tail, and from the top of the head to the feet. Apply dog shampoo as directed on the bottle, but avoid the face while doing so to prevent any irritation to the sensitive eyes. The face is cleansed easily using a damp face flannel. There are a vast number of shampoo formulations available for dogs, some of which are medicated for use with specific coat and skin problems. The mildest shampoo is often the best to avoid stripping the coat of essential oils, particularly in liver-coloured coats.

Work the shampoo all the way down to the skin. You can use this opportunity to check the skin for any bumps, bites or other abnormalities. Do not neglect any area of the body—get all of the hard-to-reach places. After thoroughly lathering the dog, paying attention to the leg, belly and ear feathering, the dog should be rinsed thoroughly with tepid water. A spray device, such as used for showering, makes the job of rinsing the dog much easier to do. Once again, be careful that no shampoo or soapy water gets near the dog's eyes. It is essential that all traces of shampoo be removed, as leaving any shampoo in the coat will attract dirt as well as potentially irritate the skin.

When removing your Sussex from the bath, be prepared for him

BATHING BEAUTY
Once you are sure that the dog is thoroughly rinsed, squeeze the excess water out of his coat with your hand and dry him with an heavy towel to remove the initial moisture. Finish the job with a blaster on low heat. In cold weather, never allow your dog outside with a wet coat.

There are 'dry bath' products on the market, which are sprays and powders intended for spot cleaning, that can be used between regular baths if necessary. They are not substitutes for regular baths, but they are easy to use for touch-ups as they do not require rinsing.

to shake out his coat—you might want to stand back, but make sure you have an hold on the dog to keep him from running through the house. Following rinsing, it is essential to dry the haircoat. An hand-held blaster on the low heat setting works quite well. Take care to direct the flow of air away from the face and to maintain a safe distance between the blaster and the dog. When the coat is dry, use the bristle brush for the body coat and use the comb to smooth out the feathering.

It is helpful to apply a coat conditioner, according to package directions, to accompany the final brushing after drying the dog. Just as a conditioning rinse is helpful to styling your own hair without tangles, coat conditioner works with the Sussex Spaniel's feathering.

EAR CLEANING

The beautiful ears of the Sussex Spaniel do require routine care. Routine care of the ears goes a long way toward preventing ear infections in this breed with pendulous ears, as the weight and length of the ears effectively cloak the ear openings, thereby creating an ideal dark, moist environment for infection. Ears should be cleaned weekly, using cotton wipes and a powder or liquid cleansing agent as recommended by your vet or breeder. Do not be tempted to use a cotton bud rather than the cotton wipe. It is far too easy to probe too deeply with a cotton bud and cause harm.

It is recommended that the hair around the ear openings be shortened by plucking or careful use of a thinning shear. This will keep the ear as dry as possible, particularly for Sussex Spaniels who will do a bit of swimming.

NAIL CLIPPING

Sussex Spaniels generally have tough, dark toenails and the 'quick' (vascular nail bed) is nearly impossible to see. Nails must be maintained on a weekly basis, as nails that are too long may result in improper placement of the foot as the nail hits the

Clean carefully around the eyes to remove any dirt or debris that can collect there, using a soft wipe and special cleanser.

Never probe into the ear canal. Clean your Sussex Spaniel's outer ears with a cotton wipe and ear powder or liquid made for dogs.

Weekly brushing of your Sussex Spaniel's teeth between visits to the vet is highly recommended.

In addition to nail care, trimming the hair between the footpads will add to the foot's neat appearance as well as the dog's comfort.

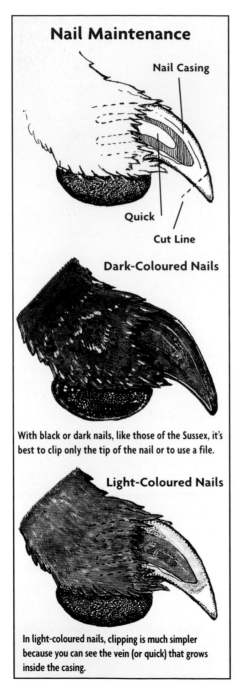

Nail Maintenance

Nail Casing

Quick

Cut Line

Dark-Coloured Nails

With black or dark nails, like those of the Sussex, it's best to clip only the tip of the nail or to use a file.

Light-Coloured Nails

In light-coloured nails, clipping is much simpler because you can see the vein (or quick) that grows inside the casing.

floor. A nail clipper is used to nip off the end of the nail, followed by using a nail file to smooth rough edges. Styptic powder is a necessity since, with the difficulty of seeing where the nail bed is, it is all too easy to cut a bit too close. As an alternative, a nail grinder may be utilised to shorten the nail while providing the same smoothing effect of the file at the same time.

Many dogs dislike nail cutting intensely. This may be avoided by routinely handling the feet at times other than nail cutting. Also, your Sussex Spaniel should be accustomed to having his nails trimmed at an early age, since nail clipping will be a part of your maintenance routine throughout his life. If the puppy is accustomed to the procedure, he should grow up to tolerate it as an adult.

TOOTH CARE

Tartar build-up can be problematic, so routine care of the mouth is important to prevent tooth decay and gum disease. Weekly attention to the teeth is helpful in maintaining the teeth in the best possible manner. While providing chew bones is helpful for removing tartar build-up naturally as the dog gnaws, this is not sufficient on its own.

TRAVELLING WITH YOUR DOG

CAR TRAVEL

You should accustom your Sussex Spaniel to riding in a car at an early age. You may or may not take him in the car often, but at the very least he will need to go to the vet and you do not want these trips to be traumatic for the dog or troublesome for you. The safest way for a dog to ride in the car is in his crate. If he uses a crate in the house, you can use the same crate for travel.

Put the pup in the crate and see how he reacts. If he seems uneasy, you can have a passenger hold him on his lap while you drive. Another option for car travel is a specially made safety harness for dogs, which straps the dog in much like a seat belt. Do not let the dog roam loose in the vehicle—this is very dangerous! If you should stop short, your dog can be thrown and injured. If the dog starts climbing on you and pestering you while you are driving, you will not be able to concentrate on the road. It is an unsafe

PEDICURE TIP

A dog that spends a lot of time outside on an hard surface, such as cement or pavement, will have his nails naturally worn down and may not need to have them trimmed as often, except maybe in the colder months when he is not outside as much. Regardless, it is best to get your dog accustomed to the nail-trimming procedure at an early age so that he is used to it. Some dogs are especially sensitive about having their feet touched, but if a dog has experienced it since puppyhood, it should not bother him.

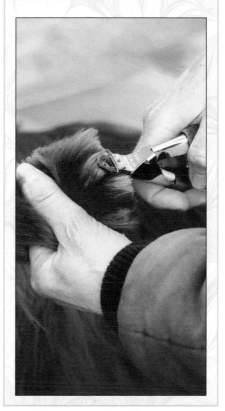

situation for everyone—human and canine.

For long trips, be prepared to stop to let the dog relieve himself. Take with you whatever you need to clean up after him, including some paper kitchen towels and perhaps some old towelling for use should he have a toileting accident in the car or suffer from travel sickness.

AIR TRAVEL

While it is possible to take a dog on a flight within Britain, this is fairly unusual and advance permission is always required. The dog will be required to travel in a fibreglass crate and you should always check in advance with the airline regarding specific requirements. To help put the dog at ease, give him one of his favourite toys in the crate. Do not feed the dog for several hours before arriving at the airport in order to minimise his need to relieve himself. However, certain regulations specify that water must always be made available to the dog in the crate.

Make sure your dog is properly identified and that your contact information appears on his ID tags and on his crate. Animals travel in a different area of the aeroplane from human passengers, so every rule must be strictly followed so as to prevent the risk of getting separated from your dog.

BOARDING

So you want to take a family holiday—and you want to include *all* members of the family. You would probably make arrangements for accommodation ahead of time anyway, but this is especially important when travelling with a dog. You do not want to make an overnight stop at the only place around for miles, only to find out that they do not allow dogs. Also, you do not want to reserve a place for your family without confirming that you are travelling with a dog, because, if it is against their policy, you may end up without a place to stay.

CONSIDERATIONS ABOUT BOARDING

Will your dog be exercised at least twice a day? How often during the day will the staff keep him company? Does the kennel provide a clean and secure environment? These are some of the questions you should consider when choosing a boarding kennel.

Likewise, if the staff asks you a lot of questions, this is a good sign. They need to know your dog's personality and temperament, health record, special requirements and what commands he has learned. Above all, follow your instincts. If you have a bad feeling about a kennel, even if a friend has recommended it, don't put your dog in its care.

Visit local boarding kennels to find one that suits your needs and with which you feel comfortable. Perhaps your vet or breeder has boarding facilities or can recommend a suitable kennel.

Alternatively, if you are travelling and choose not to bring your Sussex Spaniel, you will have to make arrangements for him while you are away. Some options are to take him to a neighbour's house to stay while you are gone, to have a trusted neighbour pop in often or stay at your house or to take your dog to a reputable boarding kennel. If you choose to board him at a kennel, you should visit in advance to see the facilities provided and where the dogs are kept. Are the dogs' areas spacious and kept clean? Talk to some of the employees and see how they treat the dogs—do they spend time with the dogs, play with them, exercise them, etc.? Also find out the kennel's policy on vaccinations and what they require. This is for all of the dogs' safety, since there is a greater risk

of diseases being passed from dog to dog when dogs are kept together.

IDENTIFICATION
Your Sussex Spaniel is your valued companion and friend. That is why you always keep a close eye on him and you have made sure that he cannot escape from the garden or wriggle out of his collar and run away from you. However, accidents can happen and there may come a time when your dog unexpectedly becomes separated from you. If this unfortunate event should occur, the first thing on your mind will be finding him. Proper identification, including an ID tag, a tattoo and possibly a microchip, will increase the chances of his being returned to you safely and quickly.

TRAINING YOUR
SUSSEX SPANIEL

Living with an untrained dog is a lot like owning a piano that you do not know how to play—it is a nice object to look at, but it does not do much more than that to bring you pleasure. Now try taking piano lessons, and suddenly the piano comes alive and brings forth magical sounds and rhythms that set your heart singing and your body swaying.

The same is true with your Sussex Spaniel. Any dog is a big responsibility and, if not trained sensibly, may develop unaccept-able behaviour that annoys you or could even cause family friction.

To train your Sussex Spaniel, you may like to enrol in an obedience class. Teach your dog good manners as you learn how and why he behaves the way he does. Find out how to communi-cate with your dog and how to recognise and understand his communications with you. Suddenly the dog takes on a new role in your life—he is clever, interesting, well behaved and fun to be with. He demonstrates his bond of devotion to you daily. In other words, your Sussex Spaniel does wonders for your ego

because he constantly reminds you that you are not only his leader, you are his hero!

Those involved with teaching dog obedience and counselling owners about their dogs' behaviour have discovered some interesting facts about dog

ownership. For example, training dogs when they are puppies results in the highest rate of success in developing well-mannered and well-adjusted adult dogs. Training an older dog, from six months to six years of age, can produce almost equal results, providing that the owner accepts the dog's slower rate of learning capability and is willing to work patiently to help the dog succeed at developing to his fullest potential. Unfortunately, many owners of untrained adult dogs lack the patience factor, so they do not persist until their dogs are successful at learning particular behaviours.

Training a puppy aged 10 to 16 weeks (20 weeks at the most) is like working with a dry sponge in a pool of water. The pup soaks up whatever you show him and constantly looks for more things to do and learn. At this early age, his body is not yet producing hormones, and therein lies the reason for such an high rate of success. Without hormones, he is focused on his owners and not particularly interested in investigating other places, dogs, people, etc. You are his leader: his provider of food, water, shelter and security. He latches onto you and wants to stay close. He will usually follow you from room to room, will not let you out of his sight when you are outdoors with him and will respond in like manner to the people and animals you encounter. If you greet a friend warmly, he will be happy to greet the person as well. If, however, you are hesitant or anxious about the approach of a stranger, he will respond accordingly.

Once the puppy begins to produce hormones, his natural curiosity emerges and he begins to investigate the world around him. It is at this time when you may notice that the untrained dog begins to wander away from you and even ignore your commands

All members of the family should take part in the Sussex Spaniel's training, to ensure that the dog will obey no matter who gives the commands.

to stay close. When this behaviour becomes a problem, you have two choices: get rid of the dog or train him. It is strongly urged that you choose the latter option.

You usually will be able to find obedience classes within a reasonable distance from your home, but you can also do a lot to train your dog yourself. Sometimes there are classes available, but the tuition is too costly. Whatever the circumstances, the solution to training your dog without obedience classes lies within the pages of this book.

This chapter is devoted to helping you train your Sussex Spaniel at home. If the recommended procedures are followed faithfully, you may expect positive results that will prove rewarding both to you and your dog. Sussex Spaniels taught systematically and fairly have no predilection for difficulty with any command. Systematic and fair education that lays a good base upon which all other training is built is essential.

Whether your new charge is a puppy or a mature adult, the methods of teaching and the techniques we use in training basic behaviours are the same. After all, no dog, whether puppy or adult, likes harsh or inhumane methods. The Sussex Spaniel will not react well to harsh training, but he will respond favourably to gentle motivational methods and sincere praise and encouragement. The reinforcement of praise from his owner and the approval that praise conveys are of utmost importance as befits his loyalty to his owner. Now let us get started.

REAP THE REWARDS

If you start with a normal, healthy dog and give him time, patience and some carefully executed lessons, you will reap the rewards of that training for the life of the dog. And what a life it will be! The two of you will find immeasurable pleasure in the companionship you have built together with love, respect and understanding.

HOUSE-TRAINING

You can train a puppy to relieve himself wherever you choose, but this must be somewhere suitable. You should bear in mind from the outset that when your puppy is old enough to go out in public places, any canine deposits must be removed at once. You will always have to carry with you a small plastic bag or 'poop-scoop.'

Outdoor training includes such surfaces as grass, soil and cement. Indoor training usually means training your dog to newspaper. When deciding on the surface and location that you will want your Sussex Spaniel to use, be sure it is going to be permanent. Training your dog to grass and then changing your mind a few months later is extremely difficult for both dog and owner.

Next, choose the command you will use each and every time you want your puppy to void. 'Hurry up' and 'Toilet' are examples of commands com -monly used by dog owners. Get in

the habit of giving the puppy your chosen relief command before you take him out. That way, when he becomes an adult, you will be able to determine if he wants to go out when you ask him. A confirmation will be signs of interest, such as wagging his tail, watching you intently, going to the door, etc.

Accustom your pup to his lead and collar and start taking him to his relief area right away. Your pup can't tell you when it's time 'to go,' so it's best to err on the side of caution.

PUPPY'S NEEDS

The puppy needs to relieve himself after play periods, after each meal, after he has been sleeping and at any time he indicates that he is looking for a place to urinate or defecate. The urinary and intestinal tract muscles of very young puppies are not fully developed. There-fore, like human babies, puppies need to relieve themselves frequently.

Take your puppy out often— every hour for an eight-week-old pup, for example—and always immediately after sleeping and

---

THINK BEFORE YOU BARK

Dogs are sensitive to their masters' moods and emotions. Use your voice wisely when communicating with your dog. Never raise your voice at your dog unless you are trying to correct him. 'Barking' at your dog can become as meaningless as 'dogspeak' is to you.

CANINE DEVELOPMENT TIMETABLE

It is important to understand how and at what age a puppy develops into adulthood.
If you are a puppy owner, consult the following Canine Development Timetable to
determine the stage of development your puppy is currently experiencing.
This knowledge will help you as you work with the puppy in the weeks and months ahead.

Period	Age	Characteristics
FIRST TO THIRD	BIRTH TO SEVEN WEEKS	Puppy needs food, sleep and warmth, and responds to simple and gentle touching. Needs mother for security and disciplining. Needs littermates for learning and interacting with other dogs. Pup learns to function within a pack and learns pack order of dominance. Begin socialising with adults and children for short periods. Begins to become aware of his environment.
FOURTH	EIGHT TO TWELVE WEEKS	Brain is fully developed. Needs socialising with outside world. Remove from mother and littermates. Needs to change from canine pack to human pack. Human dominance necessary. Fear period occurs between 8 and 12 weeks. Avoid fright and pain.
FIFTH	THIRTEEN TO SIXTEEN WEEKS	Training and formal obedience should begin. Less association with other dogs, more with people, places, situations. Period will pass easily if you remember this is pup's change-to-adolescence time. Be firm and fair. Flight instinct prominent. Permissiveness and over-disciplining can do permanent damage. Praise for good behaviour.
JUVENILE	FOUR TO EIGHT MONTHS	Another fear period about 7 to 8 months of age. It passes quickly, but be cautious of fright and pain. Sexual maturity reached. Dominant traits established. Dog should understand sit, down, come and stay by now.

NOTE: THESE ARE APPROXIMATE TIME FRAMES. ALLOW FOR INDIVIDUAL DIFFERENCES IN PUPPIES.

eating. The older the puppy, the less often he will need to relieve himself. Finally, as a mature healthy adult, he will require only three to five relief trips per day.

HOUSING

Since the types of housing and control you provide for your puppy have a direct relationship on the success of house-training, we consider the various aspects of both before we begin training.

Taking a new puppy home and turning him loose in your house can be compared to turning a child loose in a sports arena and telling the child that the place is all his! The sheer enormity of the place would be too much for him to handle. Instead, offer the puppy clearly defined areas where he can play, sleep, eat and live. A room of the house where the family gathers is the most obvious choice. Puppies are social animals

> **PARENTAL GUIDANCE**
> Training a dog is a life experience. Many parents admit that much of what they know about raising children they learned from caring for their dogs. Dogs respond to love, fairness and guidance, just as children do. Become a good dog owner and you may become an even better parent.

and need to feel a part of the pack right from the start. Hearing your voice, watching you while you are doing things and smelling you nearby are all positive reinforcers that he is now a member of your pack. Usually a family room, the kitchen or a nearby adjoining breakfast area is ideal for providing safety and security for both puppy and owner.

Within the designated room,

The dog on the left got a surprise to find the toilet already in use!

TAKE THE LEAD
Do not carry your dog to his toilet area. Lead him there on a lead or, better yet, encourage him to follow you to the spot. If you start carrying him to his spot, you might end up doing this routine forever and your dog will have the satisfaction of having trained *you*.

there should be a smaller area that the puppy can call his own. An alcove, a wire or fibreglass dog crate or a fenced (not boarded!) corner from which he can view the activities of his new family will be fine. The size of the area or crate is the key factor here. The area must be large enough so that the puppy can lie down and stretch out, as well as sit up, without rubbing his head on the top. At the same time, it must be small enough so that he cannot relieve himself at one end and sleep at the other without coming into contact with his droppings

before he is fully trained to relieve himself outside. Dogs are, by nature, clean animals and will not remain close to their relief areas unless forced to do so. In those cases, they then become dirty dogs and usually remain that way for life.

The dog's designated area should contain clean bedding and a toy. Water must always be available, in a non-spill container, although it's not advised to put water in the pup's crate until house-training has been achieved reliably.

CONTROL
By *control*, we mean helping the puppy to create a lifestyle pattern that will be compatible to that of his human pack (YOU!). Just as we guide little children to learn our way of life, we must show the puppy when it is time to play, eat, sleep, exercise and even entertain himself.

Your puppy should always sleep in his crate. He should also learn that, during times of household confusion and excessive human activity, such as at breakfast when family members are preparing for the day, he can play by himself in relative safety and comfort in his designated area. Each time you leave the puppy alone, he should understand exactly where he is to stay.

Puppies are chewers. They cannot tell the difference between lamp and television leads, shoes, table legs, etc. Chewing into a television lead, for example, can be fatal to the puppy, while a shorted wire can start a fire in the house. If the puppy chews on the arm of the chair when he is alone, you will probably discipline him angrily when you get home. Thus, he makes the association that your coming home means he is going to be punished. (He will not remember chewing the chair and is incapable of making the association of the discipline with his naughty deed.) Accustoming the pup to his designated area not only keeps him safe but also avoids his engaging in destructive behaviour when you are not around.

Times of excitement, such as special occasions, family parties, etc., can be fun for the puppy, providing that he can view the activities from the security of his designated area. He is not underfoot and he is not being fed all sorts of titbits that will probably cause him stomach distress, yet he still feels a part of the fun.

SCHEDULE

A puppy should be taken to his relief area each time he is released from his designated area, after meals, after a play session and when he first awakens in the morning (at age eight weeks, this can mean 5 a.m.!). The puppy will

HOW MANY TIMES A DAY?

AGE	RELIEF TRIPS
To 14 weeks	10
14–22 weeks	8
22–32 weeks	6
Adulthood (dog stops growing)	4

These are estimates, of course, but they are a guide to the *minimum* number of opportunities a dog should have each day to relieve himself.

indicate that he's ready 'to go' by circling or sniffing busily—do not misinterpret these signs. For a puppy less than ten weeks of age, a routine of taking him out every hour is necessary. As the puppy grows, he will be able to wait for longer periods of time.

Keep trips to his relief area short. Stay no more than five or six minutes and then return to the house. If he goes during that time, praise him lavishly and take him indoors immediately. If he does not, but he has an accident when you go back indoors, pick him up immediately, say 'No! No!' and return to his relief area. Wait a few minutes, then return to the house again. Never hit a puppy or put his face in urine or excrement when he has had an accident!

Once indoors, put the puppy in his crate until you have had

THE SUCCESS METHOD

6 Steps to Successful Crate Training

1 Tell the puppy 'Crate time!' and place him in the crate with a small treat (a piece of cheese or half of a biscuit). Let him stay in the crate for five minutes while you are in the same room. Then release him and praise lavishly. Never release him when he is fussing. Wait until he is quiet before you let him out.

2 Repeat Step 1 several times a day.

3 The next day, place the puppy in the crate as before. Let him stay there for ten minutes. Do this several times.

4 Continue building time in five-minute increments until the puppy stays in his crate for 30 minutes with you in the room. Always take him to his relief area after prolonged periods in his crate.

5 Now go back to Step 1 and let the puppy stay in his crate for five minutes, this time while you are out of the room.

6 Once again, build crate time in five-minute increments with you out of the room. When the puppy will stay willingly in his crate (he may even fall asleep!) for 30 minutes with you out of the room, he will be ready to stay in it for several hours at a time.

THE CLEAN LIFE

By providing sleeping and resting quarters that fit the dog, and offering frequent opportunities to relieve himself outside his quarters, the puppy quickly learns that the outdoors (or the newspaper if you are training him to paper) is the place to go when he needs to urinate or defecate. It also reinforces his innate desire to keep his sleeping quarters clean. This, in turn, helps develop the muscle control that will eventually produce a dog with clean living habits.

time to clean up his accident. Then, release him to the family area and watch him more closely than before. Chances are, his accident was a result of your not picking up his signal or waiting too long before offering him the opportunity to relieve himself. Never hold a grudge against the puppy for accidents.

Let the puppy learn that going outdoors means it is time to relieve himself, not to play. Once trained, he will be able to play indoors and out and still differentiate between the times for play versus the times for relief.

Help him develop regular hours for naps, being alone, playing by himself and just resting, all in his crate. Encourage him to entertain himself while you are busy with your activities. Let him learn that having you near is comforting, but it is not your main purpose in life to provide him with undivided attention.

Each time you put your puppy in his own area, use the same command, whatever suits best. Soon he will run to his crate or special area when he hears you say those words.

Crate training provides safety for you, the puppy and the home. It also provides the puppy with a feeling of security, and that helps the puppy achieve self-confidence and clean habits. Remember that one of the primary ingredients in house-training your puppy is control. Regardless of your lifestyle, there will always be occasions when you will need to have a place where your dog can stay and be happy and safe. Crate

THE SUCCESS METHOD

Success that comes by luck is usually short-lived. Success that comes by well-thought-out proven methods is often more easily achieved and permanent. This is the Success Method. It is designed to give you, the puppy owner, a simple yet proven way to help your puppy develop clean living habits and a feeling of security in his new environment.

training is the answer for now and in the future.

In conclusion, a few key elements are really all you need for a successful house-training method—consistency, frequency, praise, control and supervision. By following these procedures with a normal, healthy puppy, you and the puppy will soon be past the stage of 'accidents' and ready to move on to a full and rewarding life together.

ROLES OF DISCIPLINE, REWARD AND PUNISHMENT
Discipline, training one to act in accordance with rules, brings order to life. It is as simple as that. Without discipline, particularly in a group society, chaos will reign supreme and the group will eventually perish. Humans and canines are social animals and need some form of discipline in order to function effectively. They must procure food, reproduce to keep their species going and protect their home base and their young. If there were no discipline in the lives of social animals, they would eventually die from starvation and/or predation by other stronger animals.

In the case of domestic canines, discipline in their lives is needed in order for them to understand how their pack (you and other family members) functions and how they must act in order to survive.

A large humane society in an highly populated area recently surveyed dog owners regarding their satisfaction with their relationships with their dogs. People who had trained their dogs were 75% more satisfied with their pets than those who had never trained their dogs.

Dr Edward Thorndike, a noted psychologist, established *Thorndike's Theory of Learning*, which states that a behaviour that results in a pleasant event tends to be repeated. Likewise, behaviour that results in an unpleasant event tends not to be repeated. It is this theory upon which training methods are based today. For example, if you manipulate a dog to perform a specific behaviour and reward him for doing it, he is likely to do it again because he enjoyed the end result.

Occasionally, punishment, a penalty inflicted for an offence, is necessary. The best type of punishment often comes from an outside source. For example, a child is told not to touch the cooker because he may get burned. He disobeys and touches the cooker. In doing so, he receives a burn. From that time on, he respects the heat of the cooker and avoids contact with it. Therefore, a behaviour that results in an unpleasant event tends not to be repeated.

A good example of a dog learning the hard way is the dog

who chases the house cat. He is told many times to leave the cat alone, yet he persists in teasing the cat. Then, one day, the dog begins chasing the cat but the cat turns and swipes a claw across the dog's face, leaving the dog with a painful gash on his nose. The final result is that the dog stops chasing the cat.

TRAINING EQUIPMENT

COLLAR AND LEAD
For a Sussex Spaniel, the collar and lead that you use for training must be one with which you are easily able to work, not too heavy for the dog and perfectly safe.

TREATS
Have a bag of treats on hand; something nutritious and easy to swallow works best. Use a soft treat, a chunk of cheese or a piece of cooked chicken rather than a dry biscuit. By the time the dog has finished chewing a dry treat, he will forget why he is being rewarded in the first place!

Using food rewards will not teach a dog to beg at the table—the only way to teach a dog to beg at the table is to give him food from the table. In training, rewarding the dog with a food treat will help him associate praise and the treats with learning new behaviours that obviously please his owner. The Sussex Spaniel is not as food-motivated as many breeds; he relishes praise from his owner much more. However, titbits can be helpful in getting the dog's attention and teaching new exercises, as long as you don't skimp on the praise!

TRAINING BEGINS: ASK THE DOG A QUESTION

In general, training the Sussex Spaniel must be fun for owner and dog. The Sussex is always up to a game. Care must be taken to avoid any type of training routines that are overly repetitive and boring; the intelligence of the breed demands this.

While seemingly 'unable' to hear a command at will, the Sussex often chooses when to respond. As such, much praise and positive reinforcement are necessary, as the Sussex responds to these above all else in training.

In order to teach your dog anything, you must first get his attention. After all, he cannot learn anything if he is looking

Conduct training sessions with your Sussex in a securely enclosed location, because if he should be distracted by something that he deems more interesting, he'll be off and running in no time.

> **PLAN TO PLAY**
> The puppy should also have regular play and exercise sessions when he is with you or a family member. Exercise for a very young puppy can consist of a short walk around the house or garden. Playing can include fetching games with a large ball or a special raggy. (All puppies teethe and need soft things upon which to chew.) Remember to restrict play periods to indoors within his living area (the family room, for example) until he is completely house-trained.

away from you with his mind on something else.

To get your dog's attention, ask him 'School?' and immediately walk over to him and give him a treat and praise as you tell him 'Good dog.' Wait a minute or two and repeat the routine, this time with a treat in your hand as you approach within a foot of the dog. Do not go directly to him, but stop about a foot short of him and hold out the treat as you ask 'School?' He will see you approaching with a treat in your hand and most likely begin walking toward you. As you meet, give him the treat and praise again.

The third time, ask the question, have a treat in your hand and walk only a short distance toward the dog so that he must walk almost all the way to you. As he reaches you, give him

the treat and praise again.

By this time, the dog will probably be getting the idea that if he pays attention to you, especially when you ask that question, it will pay off in praise, treats, enjoyable activities and time spent with you. In other words, he learns that 'school' means doing great things with you that are fun and that result in positive attention for him.

Remember that the dog does not understand your verbal language; he only recognises sounds. Your question translates to a series of sounds for him, and those sounds become the signal to go to you and pay attention. The dog learns that if he does this, he will get to interact with you plus receive treats and praise.

THE BASIC COMMANDS

TEACHING SIT

Now that you have the dog's attention, attach his lead and hold it in your left hand, and hold a food treat in your right

hand. Place your food hand at the dog's nose and let him lick the treat but not take it from you. Say 'Sit' and slowly raise your food hand from in front of the dog's nose up over his head so that he is looking at the ceiling. As he bends his head upward, he will have to bend his knees to maintain his balance. As he bends his knees, he will assume a sit position. At that point, release the food treat and praise lavishly with comments such as 'Good dog! Good sit!,' etc. Remember to always praise enthusiastically, because Sussex Spaniels relish verbal praise from their owners and feel so proud of

Training your Sussex Spaniel to sit upon command is a necessary exercise and one that can be achieved quite easily.

HONOUR AND OBEY

Dogs are the most honourable animals in existence. They consider another species (humans) as their own. They interface with you. You are their leader. Some Sussex perceive children to be on their level; their actions around small children are different from their behaviour around their adult masters.

themselves whenever they accomplish a behaviour.

You will not use food forever in getting the dog to obey your commands. Food is only used to teach new behaviours and, once the dog knows what you want when you give a specific command, you will wean him off the food treats but still maintain the verbal praise, which the Sussex appreciates more than a biscuit or sliver of liver.

TEACHING DOWN

Teaching the down exercise is easy when you understand how the dog perceives the down position, but it is very difficult when you do not. Dogs perceive the down position as a submissive one; therefore, teaching the down exercise by using a forceful method can sometimes make the dog develop such a fear of the down that he either runs away when you say 'Down' or he attempts to snap at the person who tries to force him down.

Have the dog sit close alongside your left leg, facing in the same direction as you are. Hold the lead in your left hand and a food treat in your right. Now place your left hand lightly on the top of the dog's shoulders where they meet above the spinal cord. Do not push down on the dog's shoulders; simply rest your left hand there so you can guide the dog to lie down close to your left leg rather than to swing away from your side when he drops.

Now place the food hand at the dog's nose, say 'Down' very softly (almost a whisper), and slowly lower the food hand to the dog's front feet. When the food hand reaches the floor, begin moving it forward along the floor in front of the dog. Keep talking softly to the dog, saying things like, 'Do you want this treat? You can do this, good dog.' Your reassuring tone of voice will help calm the dog as he tries to follow the food hand in order to get the treat.

When the dog's elbows touch the floor, release the food and praise softly. Try to get the dog to maintain that down position for several seconds before you let him get up again. The goal here is to get the dog to settle down and not feel threatened in the down position.

TEACHING STAY

It is easy to teach the dog to stay in either a sit or a down position. Again, we use food and praise during the teaching process as we help the dog to understand exactly what it is that we are expecting him to do.

To teach the sit/stay, start with the dog sitting on your left side as before and hold the lead in your left hand. Have a food treat in your right hand and place your food hand at the dog's nose. Say 'Stay' and step out on your right foot to stand directly in front of the dog, toe to toe, as he licks and nibbles the treat. Be sure to keep his head facing upward to maintain the sit position. Count to five and then swing around to stand next to the dog again with him on your left. As soon as you get back to the original position, release the food and praise lavishly.

To teach the down/stay, do the down as previously described. As soon as the dog lies down, say 'Stay' and step out on your right foot just as you did in the sit/stay.

Count to five and then return to stand beside the dog with him on your left side. Release the treat and praise as always.

Within a week or ten days, you can begin to add a bit of distance between you and your dog when you leave him. When you do, use your left hand open with the palm facing the dog as a stay signal, much the same as the hand signal a constable uses to stop traffic at a crossroads. Hold the food treat in your right hand as before, but this time the food

DOUBLE JEOPARDY

A dog in jeopardy never lies down. He stays alert on his feet because instinct tells him that he may have to run away or fight for his survival. Therefore, if a dog feels threatened or anxious, he will not lie down. Consequently, it is important to keep the dog calm and relaxed as he learns the down exercise.

One of the biggest challenges in training is keeping the student focused and attentive. Teaching a lesson is pointless if the dog becomes bored by repetition or if his attention is elsewhere.

will not be touching the dog's nose. He will watch the food hand and quickly learn that he is going to get that treat as soon as you return to his side.

When you can stand 1 metre away from your dog for 30 seconds, you can then begin building time and distance in both stays. Eventually, the dog can be expected to remain in the stay position for prolonged periods of time until you return to him or call him to you. Always praise lavishly when he stays.

TEACHING COME
Since the Sussex has the tendency to respond to a command when he chooses, it is essential that a puppy be taught a reliable recall, or 'come,' command. Training the Sussex Spaniel to come when called as a reflex behaviour is essential and best taught as a puppy. It is for the good of the dog that a reliable recall is so important; a dog that does not reliably come when called cannot be called out of danger.

If you make teaching 'come' an exciting experience and make a game of it, you should never have a student that does not love the game or that fails to come when called. The secret, it seems, is never to use the word 'come.'

At times when an owner most

'COME' . . . BACK

Never call your dog to come to you for a correction or scold him when he reaches you. That is the quickest way to turn a Come command into 'Go away fast!' Dogs think only in the present tense, and your dog will connect the scolding with coming to you, not with the misbehaviour of a few minutes earlier.

wants his dog to come when called, the owner is likely to be upset or anxious and he allows these feelings to come through in the tone of his voice when he calls his dog. Hearing that desperation in his owner's voice, the dog fears the results of going to him and therefore either disobeys outright or runs in the opposite direction. The secret, therefore, is to teach the dog a game and, when you want him to come to you, simply play the game. It is practically a no-fail solution!

To begin, have several members of your family take a few food treats and each go into a different room in the house. Everyone takes turns calling the dog, and each person should celebrate the dog's finding him with a treat and lots of happy praise. When a person calls the dog, he is actually inviting the dog to find him and to get a treat as a reward for 'winning.'

A few turns of the 'Where are

you?' game and the dog will understand that everyone is playing the game and that each person has a big celebration awaiting the dog's success at locating him or her. Once the dog learns to love the game, simply calling out 'Where are you?' will bring him running from wherever

'WHERE ARE YOU?'

When calling the dog, do not say 'Come.' Say things like, 'Rover, where are you? See if you can find me! I have a biscuit for you!' Keep up a constant line of chatter with coaxing sounds and frequent questions such as, 'Where are you?' The dog will learn to follow the sound of your voice to locate you and receive his reward.

he is when he hears that all-important question.

The come command is recognised as one of the most important things to teach a dog, but there are trainers who work with thousands of dogs and never teach the actual word 'come.' Yet these dogs will race to respond to a person who uses the dog's name followed by 'Where are you?' For example, a woman has a 12-year-old companion dog who went blind, but who never fails to locate her owner when asked, 'Where are you?'

Children, in particular, love to play this game with their dogs. Children can hide in smaller places like a shower or bath, behind a bed or under a table. The dog needs to work a little bit harder to find these hiding places, but, when he does, he loves to celebrate with a treat and a tussle with a favourite youngster.

You'll know that you've achieved success with the come command when your Sussex runs to you this enthusiastically!

TEACHING HEEL

Heeling means that the dog walks beside the owner without pulling. It takes time and patience on the owner's part to succeed at teaching the dog that he (the owner) will not proceed unless the dog is walking calmly beside him. Neither pulling out ahead on the lead nor lagging behind is acceptable.

Begin by holding the lead in your left hand as the dog sits beside your left leg. Move the loop end of the lead to your right hand, but keep your left hand short on the lead so that it keeps the dog in close next to you.

Say 'Heel' and step forward on your left foot. Keep the dog close to you and take three steps. Stop and have the dog sit next to you in what we now call the heel position. Praise verbally, but do not touch the dog. Hesitate a moment and begin again with 'Heel,' taking three steps and stopping, at which point the dog is told to sit again.

Your goal here is to have the dog walk those three steps without pulling on the lead. Once he will walk calmly beside you for three steps without pulling, increase the number of steps you take to five. When he will walk politely beside you while you take five steps, you can increase the length of your walk to ten steps. Keep increasing the length of your stroll until the dog will

walk calmly beside you without pulling as long as you want him to heel. When you stop heeling, indicate to the dog that the exercise is over by verbally praising as you pet him and say 'OK, good dog.' The 'OK' is used as a release word, meaning that the exercise is finished and the dog is free to relax.

If you are dealing with a dog who insists on pulling you around, simply 'put on your brakes' and stand your ground until the dog realises that the two of you are not going anywhere until he is beside you and moving at your pace, not his. It may take some time just standing there to convince the dog that you are the leader and that you will be the one to decide on the direction and speed of your travel.

Each time the dog looks up at you or slows down to give a slack lead between the two of you, quietly praise him and say, 'Good heel. Good dog.' Eventually, the dog will begin to respond and within a few days he will be walking politely beside you without pulling on the lead. At first, the training sessions should be kept short and very positive; soon the dog will be able to walk nicely with you for increasingly longer distances. Remember also to give the dog free time and the opportunity to run and play when you have finished heel practice.

Make eye contact with your dog as you train him to heel and let him know what is expected of him.

With patience and practice, your Sussex will soon be right in step with you, at your pace.

The show dog takes the heel command a step further, as he must follow his handler in the ring while the judge evaluates his movement.

OBEDIENCE CLASSES

It is a good idea to enrol in an obedience class if one is available in your area. If yours is a show dog, ringcraft classes would be more appropriate. Many areas have dog clubs that offer basic obedience training as well as preparatory classes for obedience competition. There are also local dog trainers who offer similar classes.

At obedience shows, dogs can earn titles at various levels of competition. The beginning levels of obedience competition include basic behaviours such as sit, down, heel, etc. The more advanced levels of competition include jumping, retrieving, scent discrimination and signal work. Jumping may be difficult for the Sussex, with his short legs and massive body. Extreme care must be taken to avoid stress on the dog's developing skeletal structure. Jumping must be taught systematically and with care to assure good form and prevent avoidable injury, beginning with very low jump heights and progressing to any required higher heights slowly. Training of this type should not begin until the dog is at least a year old.

While the Sussex is capable of advanced obedience work, and has enjoyed considerable success in the United States, caution is necessary. The prospective owner who wishes to have an advanced competition dog for obedience may do well to reconsider their motives in

> ### WEANING OFF FOOD IN TRAINING
> Although praise is the most important motivator with the Sussex Spaniel, you will likely also use food in training new behaviours. Once the dog understands what behaviour goes with a specific command, it is time to start weaning him off the food treats. At first, give a treat after each exercise. Then, start to give a treat only after every other exercise. Mix up the times when you offer a food reward and the times when you only offer praise so that the dog will never know when he is going to receive both food and praise and when he is going to receive only praise. This is called a variable ratio reward system. It proves successful because there is always the chance that the owner will produce a treat, so the dog will keep trying for that reward. No matter what, *always* give verbal praise.

acquiring a Sussex Spaniel. If you are interested in participating in organised competition with your Sussex Spaniel, there are activities other than obedience in which you and your dog can become involved. Sussex Spaniels excel in tracking. The large nose of the Sussex is ideally suited and able to work in a variety of situations that capitalise on his purposeful and powerful scenting ability. Sussex Spaniels have been trained to use their noses in search-and-rescue work, narcotics detection and other similar endeavours in addition to being trained for participation in standard tracking tests.

Agility is a popular sport in

which dogs run through obstacle course that includes various jumps, tunnels and other exercises to test the dog's speed and coordination. Again, the jumping exercises may be difficult for the Sussex Spaniel and should only be undertaken with extreme caution. The Kennel Club requires the dog to be at least 12 months of age before training for agility. The breed is very capable of success in agility competition but, again, an owner who is choosing a dog first and foremost for agility may do well to consider a breed other than the Sussex Spaniel.

OTHER ACTIVITIES FOR LIFE
Whether a dog is trained in the structured environment of a class or alone with his owner at home, there are many activities that can bring fun and rewards to both owner and dog once they have mastered basic control. Sussex Spaniels enjoy doing activities with their owners. A trained Sussex Spaniel is a joy to live with, as training and activity provide appropriate outlets for the breed's considerable ability to learn and solve problems.

Teaching the dog to help out around the home, in the garden or on the farm provides great satisfaction to both dog and owner. In addition, the dog's help makes life a little easier for his owner and raises his stature as a valued companion to his family. It helps

FEAR AGGRESSION
Pups who are subjected to physical abuse during training commonly end up with behavioural problems as adults. One common result of abuse is fear aggression, in which a dog will lash out, bare his teeth, snarl and finally bite someone by whom he feels threatened. For example, your daughter may be playing with the dog one afternoon. As they play hide-and-seek, she backs the dog into a corner and, as she attempts to tease him playfully, he bites her hand. Examine the cause of this behaviour. Did your daughter ever hit the dog? Did someone who resembles your daughter hit or scream at the dog?

Fortunately, fear aggression is relatively easy to correct. Have your daughter engage in only positive activities with the dog, such as feeding, petting and walking. She should not give any corrections or negative feedback. If the dog still growls or cowers away from her, allow someone else to accompany them. After approximately one week, the dog should feel that he can rely on her for many positive things, and he will also be prevented from reacting fearfully towards anyone who might resemble her.

If you're interested in obedience competition, start with the basics and progress from there. Obedience exercises build on commands like the sit/stay, requiring extended periods of time and longer distances from the handler.

CONSISTENCY PAYS OFF

Dogs need consistency in their feeding times, exercise and toilet breaks, and in the verbal commands you use. If you use 'Stay' on Monday and 'Stay here, please' on Tuesday, you will confuse your dog. Don't demand perfect behaviour during training classes and then let him have the run of the house the rest of the day. Above all, lavish praise on your pet consistently every time he does something right. The more he feels he is pleasing you, the more willing he will be to learn.

give the dog a purpose by occupying his mind and providing an outlet for his energy.

Rucksacking is an exciting and healthy activity that the dog can be taught without assistance from more than his owner. The exercise of walking and climbing is good for man and dog alike, and the bond that they develop together is priceless. The rule for rucksacking with any dog is never to expect the dog to carry more than one-sixth of his body weight, though given the breed's long back and considerable weight, one-eighth is more sensible.

As a member of the Gundog group, the Sussex Spaniel is well-suited for hunting game as appropriate to the breed's size. Sussex often are used to locate and flush upland game birds, later retrieving the shot game for the handler back from land or water. Fanciers have also reported success in using Sussex Spaniels on rabbit. They are are typically tenacious and thorough in working cover. Retrieving ability varies among individuals of the breed,

with some being quite natural and others quite hopeless. Said to be relatively easy to train for the field, care must be taken not to overdo it when training the retrieve. Repetition after repetition will quickly sour a Sussex for the game. While a Sussex, like any other spaniel, may charge out of gun range, a major advantage of the Sussex afield is the breed's tendency to work close.

A number of Sussex Spaniels actively participate as therapy dogs, ranging from specially trained dogs who visit nursing homes and other group-care centres to dogs who actively provide assistance. In functioning as an assistance dog, regard must be given to the overall size of the Sussex Spaniel. For example, a Sussex is not going to make a suitable guide dog for the blind due to his more compact size, but he will do well as an hearing dog. The breed's natural affinity for humans, desire to please and problem-solving ability make the Sussex well suited to this sort of training.

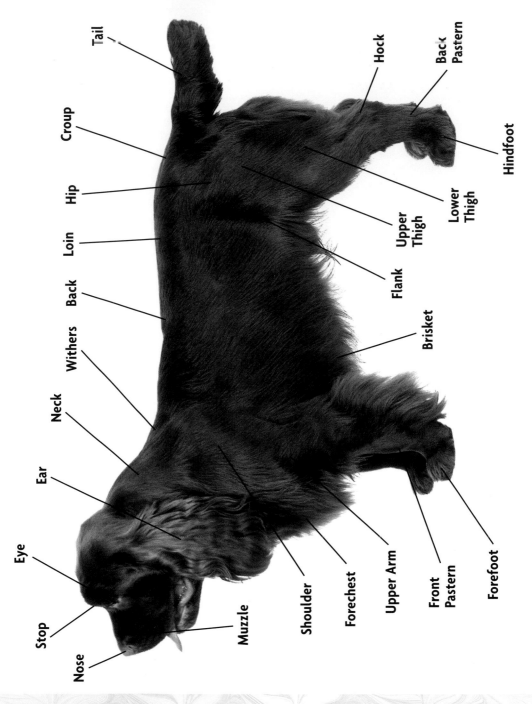

PHYSICAL STRUCTURE OF THE SUSSEX SPANIEL

Tail

Croup

Hip

Loin

Back

Withers

Neck

Ear

Eye

Stop

Nose

Muzzle

Shoulder

Forechest

Upper Arm

Front Pastern

Forefoot

Brisket

Flank

Upper Thigh

Lower Thigh

Hock

Back Pastern

Hindfoot

Dogs suffer from many of the same physical illnesses as people. They might even share many of the same psychological problems. Since people usually know more about human diseases than canine maladies, many of the terms used in this chapter will be familiar but not necessarily those used by veterinary surgeons. For example, we will use the familiar term 'x-ray' instead of 'radiograph.' We will also use the familiar term 'symptoms,' even though dogs don't have symptoms, which are verbal descriptions of something the patient feels or observes himself that he regards as abnormal. Dogs have 'clinical signs' since they cannot speak, so we have to look for these clinical signs…but we still use the term 'symptoms' in the book.

Medicine is a constantly changing art, with some scientific input as well. Things alter as we learn more and more about basic sciences such as genetics and biochemistry, and have use of more sophisticated imaging techniques like Computer Aided Tomography (CAT scans) or Magnetic Resonance Imaging (MRI scans). There is academic dispute about many canine maladies, so different veterinary surgeons treat them in different ways, and some vets have a greater emphasis on surgical techniques than others.

SELECTING A VETERINARY SURGEON

Your selection of a veterinary surgeon should be based on personal recommendation for his skills with small animals, especially dogs, and, if possible, especially spaniel breeds. If the vet is based nearby, it will be helpful because you might have an emergency or need to make multiple visits for treatments.

All veterinary surgeons are licenced, and in Britain are Members of the Royal College of Veterinary Surgeons (MRCVS after their name). The high street veterinary practice deals with routine medical issues such as infections, injuries and the promotion of health (for example, by vaccination). If the problem affecting your dog is more complex, in Britain your vet will refer your pet to someone with a

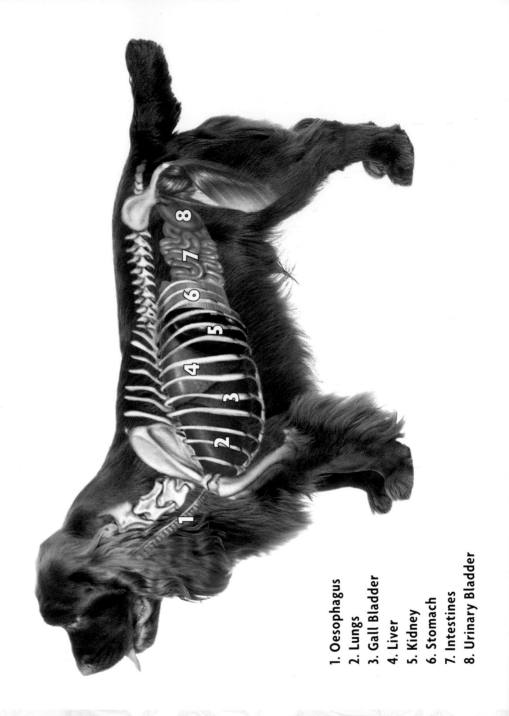

1. Oesophagus
2. Lungs
3. Gall Bladder
4. Liver
5. Kidney
6. Stomach
7. Intestines
8. Urinary Bladder

INTERNAL ORGANS OF THE SUSSEX SPANIEL

more detailed knowledge of what is wrong. This will usually be a specialist at the nearest university veterinary school who is a veterinary dermatologist, veterinary ophthalmologist, etc; whatever is the relevant field.

Veterinary procedures are very costly and as the treatments available improve, they are going to become more expensive. It is quite acceptable to discuss matters of cost with your vet; if there is more than one treatment option, cost may be a factor in deciding which route to take.

Insurance against veterinary cost is also becoming very popular. This will not pay for routine vaccinations, but will cover the costs for unexpected emergencies such as emergency surgery after a road-traffic accident.

PREVENTATIVE MEDICINE

It is much easier, less costly and more effective to practise preventative medicine than to fight bouts of illness and disease. Properly bred puppies of all breeds come from parents that were selected based upon their genetic-disease profiles. The puppies' mother should have been vaccinated, free of all internal and external parasites and properly nourished. For these reasons, a visit to the veterinary surgeon who cared for the dam is recommended if at all possible. The dam passes disease

Breakdown of Veterinary Income by Category

Dentistry

Radiology

Surgery

Vaccinations

Laboratory

Examinations

Medicines

resistance to her puppies, which should last from eight to ten weeks. Unfortunately, she can also pass on parasites and infection. This is why knowledge about her health is useful in learning more about the health of the puppies.

A typical American vet's income, categorised according to services performed. This survey dealt with small-animal (pets) practices.

WEANING TO FIVE MONTHS OLD

Puppies should be weaned by the time they are two months old. A puppy that remains for at least eight weeks with his dam and littermates usually adapts better to other dogs and people later in life.

Some new owners have their puppy examined by a veterinary surgeon immediately, which is a good idea unless the puppy is overtired by a long journey. Vaccination programmes usually begin when the puppy is very young.

The puppy will have his teeth

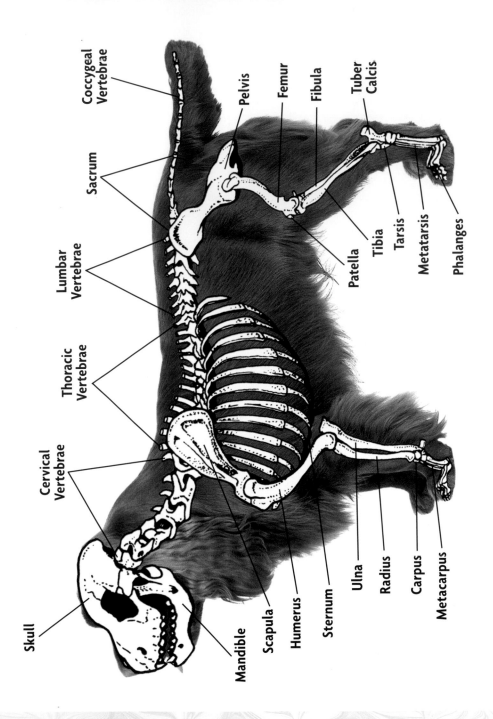

Coccygeal Vertebrae

Pelvis

Femur

Fibula

Tuber Calcis

Sacrum

Tibia

Patella

Tarsis

Metatarsis

Phalanges

Lumbar Vertebrae

Thoracic Vertebrae

Cervical Vertebrae

Skull

Mandible

Scapula

Humerus

Sternum

Ulna

Radius

Carpus

Metacarpus

SKELETAL STRUCTURE OF THE SUSSEX SPANIEL

examined and have his skeletal conformation and general health checked prior to certification by the veterinary surgeon. Puppies in certain breeds have problems with their kneecaps, cataracts and other eye problems, heart murmurs and undescended testicles. They may also have personality problems and your veterinary surgeon might have training in temperament evaluation.

VACCINATION PROGRAMME

Most vaccinations are given by injection and should only be given by a veterinary surgeon. Both he and you should keep a record of the date of the injection, the identification of the vaccine and the amount given. Some vets give a first vaccination at six weeks, but most dog breeders prefer the course not to commence until about eight to ten weeks because of interaction with the antibodies produced by the mother. The vaccination timetable is usually based on a 15-day cycle. You must take your vet's advice as to when to vaccinate, as this may differ according to the vaccine used.

The usual vaccines contain immunising doses of several different viruses such as

HEALTH AND VACCINATION TIMETABLE

AGE IN WEEKS:	6TH	8TH	10TH	12TH	14TH	16TH	20-24TH	52ND
Worm Control	✔	✔	✔	✔	✔	✔	✔	
Neutering								✔
Heartworm		✔		✔		✔	✔	
Parvovirus	✔		✔		✔		✔	✔
Distemper		✔		✔		✔		✔
Hepatitis		✔		✔		✔		✔
Leptospirosis								✔
Parainfluenza	✔		✔		✔			✔
Dental Examination		✔					✔	✔
Complete Physical		✔					✔	✔
Coronavirus				✔			✔	✔
Kennel Cough	✔							
Hip Dysplasia								✔
Rabies							✔	

Vaccinations are not instantly effective. It takes about two weeks for the dog's immune system to develop antibodies. Most vaccinations require annual booster shots. Your veterinary surgeon should guide you in this regard.

Normal hairs of a dog enlarged 200 times original size. The cuticle (outer covering) is clean and healthy. Unlike human hair that grows from the base, a dog's hair also grows from the end. Damaged hairs and split ends, illustrated above.

distemper, parvovirus, parainfluenza and hepatitis. There are other vaccines available when the puppy is at risk. You should rely upon professional advice. This is especially true for the booster immunisations. Most vaccination programmes require a booster when the puppy is a year old and once a year thereafter. In some cases, circumstances may require more or less frequent immunisations.

Kennel cough, more formally known as tracheobronchitis, is immunised against with a vaccine that is sprayed into the dog's nostrils. Kennel cough is usually included in routine vaccination, but it is often not as effective as the vaccines for other major diseases.

FIVE MONTHS TO ONE YEAR OF AGE
Unless you intend to breed or show your dog, neutering the puppy at six months of age is recommended. Discuss this with your veterinary surgeon. Neutering/ spaying has proven to be extremely beneficial to male and female puppies, respectively. Besides eliminating the possibility of pregnancy, it inhibits (but does

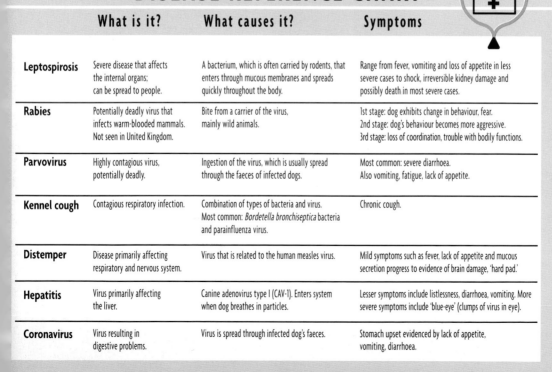

DISEASE REFERENCE CHART

	What is it?	What causes it?	Symptoms
Leptospirosis	Severe disease that affects the internal organs; can be spread to people.	A bacterium, which is often carried by rodents, that enters through mucous membranes and spreads quickly throughout the body.	Range from fever, vomiting and loss of appetite in less severe cases to shock, irreversible kidney damage and possibly death in most severe cases.
Rabies	Potentially deadly virus that infects warm-blooded mammals. Not seen in United Kingdom.	Bite from a carrier of the virus, mainly wild animals.	1st stage: dog exhibits change in behaviour, fear. 2nd stage: dog's behaviour becomes more aggressive. 3rd stage: loss of coordination, trouble with bodily functions.
Parvovirus	Highly contagious virus, potentially deadly.	Ingestion of the virus, which is usually spread through the faeces of infected dogs.	Most common: severe diarrhoea. Also vomiting, fatigue, lack of appetite.
Kennel cough	Contagious respiratory infection.	Combination of types of bacteria and virus. Most common: *Bordetella bronchiseptica* bacteria and parainfluenza virus.	Chronic cough.
Distemper	Disease primarily affecting respiratory and nervous system.	Virus that is related to the human measles virus.	Mild symptoms such as fever, lack of appetite and mucous secretion progress to evidence of brain damage, 'hard pad.'
Hepatitis	Virus primarily affecting the liver.	Canine adenovirus type I (CAV-1). Enters system when dog breathes in particles.	Lesser symptoms include listlessness, diarrhoea, vomiting. More severe symptoms include 'blue-eye' (clumps of virus in eye).
Coronavirus	Virus resulting in digestive problems.	Virus is spread through infected dog's faeces.	Stomach upset evidenced by lack of appetite, vomiting, diarrhoea.

not prevent) breast cancer in bitches and prostate cancer in male dogs. Under no circumstances should a bitch be spayed prior to her first season.

Your veterinary surgeon should provide your puppy with a thorough dental evaluation at six months of age, ascertaining whether all the permanent teeth have erupted properly. An home dental-care regimen should be initiated at six months, including brushing weekly and providing good dental devices (such as nylon bones). Regular dental care promotes healthy teeth, fresh breath and a longer life.

DOGS OLDER THAN ONE YEAR
Continue to visit the veterinary surgeon at least once a year. There is no such disease as 'old age,' but bodily functions do change with age. The eyes and ears are no longer as efficient. Liver, kidney and intestinal functions often decline. Proper dietary changes, recommended by your veterinary surgeon, can make life more pleasant for your ageing Sussex Spaniel and you.

SKIN PROBLEMS
Veterinary surgeons are consulted by dog owners for skin problems more than for any other group of diseases or maladies. A dog's skin is as sensitive, if not more so, than human skin, and both suffer from almost the same ailments

(though the occurrence of acne in dogs is rare!). For this reason, veterinary dermatology has developed into a speciality practised by many veterinary surgeons.

Since many skin problems have visual symptoms that are almost identical, it requires the skill of an experienced veterinary dermatologist to identify and cure many of the more severe skin disorders. Pet shops sell many treatments for skin problems, but most of the treatments are directed at symptoms and not at the underlying problem(s). If your dog is suffering from a skin disorder, you should seek professional assistance as quickly as possible. As with all diseases, the earlier a problem is identified and treated, the more likely that the cure will be successful.

HEREDITARY SKIN DISORDERS
Veterinary dermatologists are currently researching a number of skin disorders that are believed to have an hereditary basis. These inherited diseases are transmitted by both parents, who appear (phenotypically) normal but have a recessive gene for the disease, meaning that they carry, but are not affected by, the disease. These diseases pose serious problems to breeders because in some instances there are no methods of identifying carriers. Often the secondary diseases associated with these skin

conditions are even more debilitating than the skin disorders themselves, including cancers and respiratory problems.

Among the hereditary skin disorders, for which the mode of inheritance is known, are acrodermatitis, cutaneous asthenia (Ehlers-Danlos syndrome), sebaceous adenitis, cyclic hematopoiesis, dermatomyositis, IgA deficiency, colour dilution alopaecia and nodular dermatofibrosis. Some of these disorders are limited to one or two breeds, while others affect a large number of breeds. All inherited diseases must be diagnosed and treated by a veterinary specialist.

PARASITE BITES

Many of us are allergic to insect bites. The bites itch, erupt and may even become infected. Dogs have the same reaction to fleas, ticks and/or mites. When an insect lands on you, you have the chance to whisk it away with your hand. Unfortunately, when a dog is bitten by a flea, tick or mite, it can only scratch it away or bite it. By the time the dog has been bitten, the parasite has done some of its damage. It may also have laid eggs, which will cause further problems in the near future. The itching from parasite bites is probably due to the saliva injected into the site when the parasite sucks the dog's blood.

Time spent outdoors is enjoyable for dog and owner, but be aware of the allergens, insects and other irritants that your dog can encounter. Always check his skin and coat carefully and report any abnormalities to your vet.

AIRBORNE ALLERGIES

Just as humans have hay fever from which they suffer during the pollinating season, many dogs suffer from the same allergies. When the pollen count is high, your dog might suffer but don't expect him to sneeze and have a runny nose as a human would. Dogs react to pollen allergies in the same way they react to fleas—they scratch and bite themselves.

Dogs, like humans, can be tested for allergens. Discuss the testing with your veterinary surgeon.

ACRAL LICK GRANULOMA

Many breeds of dog have a very poorly understood syndrome called acral lick granuloma. The manifestation of the problem is the dog's tireless attack at a specific area of the body, almost always the legs or paws. The dog licks so intensively that he removes the hair and skin, leaving an ugly, large wound. Tiny protuberances, which are outgrowths of new capillaries, bead on the surface of the wound. Owners who notice their dogs' biting and chewing at their extremities should have the vet determine the cause. If lick granuloma is identified, although there is no absolute cure, corticosteroids are the most common treatment.

AUTO-IMMUNE ILLNESSES

An auto-immune illness is one in which the immune system overacts and does not recognise parts of the affected person (or dog); rather, the immune system starts to react as if these parts were foreign and need to be destroyed. An example is rheumatoid arthritis, which occurs when the body does not recognise the joints, thus leading to a very painful and damaging reaction in the joints. This has nothing to do with age, so can occur in children. The wear-and-tear arthritis of the older person or dog is osteoarthritis.

Lupus is an auto-immune disease that affects dogs as well as people. It can take variable forms, affecting the kidneys, bones and the skin. It can be fatal, so is treated with steroids, which can themselves have very significant side effects. The steroids calm down the allergic reaction to the body's tissues, which helps the lupus, but also decreases the body's reaction to real foreign substances such as bacteria, and also thins the skin and bone.

FOOD PROBLEMS

FOOD ALLERGIES

Dogs are allergic to many foods that are best-sellers and highly recommended by breeders and veterinary surgeons. Changing the brand of food that you buy may not eliminate the problem if the element to which the dog is allergic is contained in the new brand.

Recognising a food allergy can be difficult. Humans often have rashes when they eat foods to which they are allergic, or have swelling of the lips or eyes. Dogs do not usually develop rashes, but react in the same way as they do to an airborne or bite allergy—they itch, scratch and bite. While pollen allergies and parasite bites are usually seasonal, pollen allergies are year-round problems.

PET ADVANTAGES

If you do not intend to show or breed your new puppy, your veterinary surgeon will probably recommend that you spay your female or neuter your male. Some people believe neutering leads to weight gain, but if you feed and exercise your dog properly, this is easily avoided. Spaying or neutering can actually have many positive outcomes, such as:

• training becomes easier, as the dog focuses less on the urge to mate and more on you!

• females are protected from unplanned pregnancy as well as ovarian and uterine cancers.

• males are guarded from testicular tumours and have a reduced risk of developing prostate cancer.

Talk to your vet regarding the right age to spay/neuter and other aspects of the procedure.

TREATING FOOD ALLERGY

Diagnosis of food allergy is based on a two- to four-week dietary trial with an home-cooked diet fed to the exclusion of all other foods. The diet should consist of boiled rice or potato with a source of protein that the dog has never eaten before, such as fresh or frozen fish, lamb or even something as exotic as pheasant. Water has to be the only drink, and it is really important that no other foods are fed during this trial. If the dog's condition improves, you will need to try the original diet once again to see if the itching resumes. If it does, then this confirms the diagnosis that the dog is allergic to his original diet. The treatment is long-term feeding of something that does not distress the dog's skin, which may be in the form of one of the commercially available hypoallergenic diets or the home-made diet that you created for the allergy trial.

FOOD INTOLERANCE

Food intolerance is the inability of the dog to completely digest certain foods. This occurs because the dog does not have the chemicals necessary to digest some foodstuffs. These chemicals are called enzymes. All puppies have the enzymes necessary to digest canine milk, but some dogs do not have the enzymes to digest a very different form of milk that is commonly found in human households—milk from cows. In such dogs, drinking cows' milk results in loose bowels, stomach pains and the passage of gas.

Dogs often do not have the enzymes to digest soya or other beans. The treatment is to exclude the foodstuffs that upset your Sussex Spaniel's digestion.

A male dog flea,
Ctenocephalides canis.

EXTERNAL PARASITES

FLEAS

Of all the problems to which dogs are prone, none is more well known and frustrating than fleas. Flea infestation is relatively simple to cure but difficult to prevent. Parasites that are harboured inside the body are a bit more difficult to eradicate but they are easier to control.

To control flea infestation, you have to understand the flea's life cycle. Fleas are often thought of as a summertime problem, but centrally heated homes have changed the patterns and fleas can be found at any time of the year.

The most effective method of flea control is a two-stage approach: one stage to kill the adult fleas, and the other to control the development of pre-adult fleas. Unfortunately, no single active ingredient is effective against all stages of the life cycle.

LIFE CYCLE STAGES

During its life, a flea will pass through four life stages: egg, larva, pupa and adult. The adult stage is the most visible and irritating stage of the flea life cycle, and this is why the majority of flea-control products concentrate on this stage. The fact is that adult fleas account for only 1% of the total flea population, and the other 99% exist in pre-adult stages, i.e. eggs, larvae and pupae. The pre-adult stages are barely visible to the naked eye.

THE LIFE CYCLE OF THE FLEA

Eggs are laid on the dog, usually in quantities of about 20 or 30, several times a day. The adult female flea must have a blood meal before each egg-laying session. When first laid, the eggs will cling to the dog's hair, as the eggs are still moist. However, they will quickly dry out and fall from the dog, especially if the dog moves around or scratches. Many eggs will fall off in the dog's favourite area or an area in which he spends a lot of time, such as his bed.

Once the eggs fall from the dog onto the carpet or furniture, they will hatch into larvae. This takes from one to ten days. Larvae are not particularly mobile and will usually travel only a few

S. E. M. BY DR DENNIS KUNKEL, UNIVERSITY OF HAWAII

Magnified head of a dog flea, *Ctenocephalides canis*, colorized for effect.

inches from where they hatch. However, they do have a tendency to move away from light and foot traffic—under furniture and behind doors are common places to find high quantities of flea larvae.

The flea larvae feed on dead organic matter, including adult flea faeces, until they are ready to change into adult fleas. Fleas will usually remain as larvae for around seven days. After this period, the larvae will pupate into protective pupae. While inside the pupae, the larvae will undergo metamorphosis and change into adult fleas. This can take as little time as a few days, but the adult fleas can remain inside the pupae waiting to hatch for up to two years. The pupae are signalled to hatch by certain stimuli, such as physical pressure—the pupae's being stepped on, heat from an animal's lying on the pupae or

FLEA-KILLER CAUTION

Flea killers are poisonous. You should not spray these toxic chemicals on areas of a dog's body that he licks, including his genitals and his face. Flea killers taken internally are a better answer, but check with your vet in case internal therapy is not advised for your dog.

The dog flea is the most common parasite found on pet dogs.

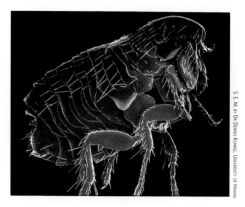

S. E. M. BY DR DENNIS KUNKEL, UNIVERSITY OF HAWAII

increased carbon-dioxide levels and vibrations—indicating that a suitable host is available.

Once hatched, the adult flea must feed within a few days. Once the adult flea finds an host, it will not leave voluntarily. It only becomes dislodged by grooming or the host animal's scratching. The adult flea will remain on the host for the duration of its life unless forcibly removed.

Dwight R Kuhn's magnificent action photo, showing a flea jumping from a dog's back.

PHOTO BY DWIGHT R KUHN

TREATING THE ENVIRONMENT AND THE DOG

Treating fleas should be a two-pronged attack. First, the environment needs to be treated; this includes carpets and furniture, especially the dog's bedding and areas underneath furniture. The environment should be treated with an household spray containing an Insect Growth Regulator (IGR) and an insecticide to kill the adult fleas. Most IGRs are effective against eggs and larvae; they actually mimic the fleas' own hormones and stop the eggs and larvae from developing into adult fleas. There are currently no treatments available to attack the pupa stage of the life cycle, so the adult insecticide is used to kill the newly hatched adult fleas before they find an host. Most IGRs are active for many months, while adult insecticides are only active for a few days.

When treating with an household spray, it is a good idea to vacuum before applying the product. This stimulates as many pupae as possible to hatch into adult fleas. The vacuum cleaner should also be treated with an insecticide to prevent the eggs and larvae that have been hoovered into the vacuum bag from hatching.

The second stage of treatment is to apply an adult insecticide to the dog. Traditionally, this would

EN GARDE:
CATCHING FLEAS OFF GUARD!

Consider the following ways to arm yourself against fleas:

- Add a small amount of pennyroyal or eucalyptus oil to your dog's bath. These natural remedies repel fleas.
- Supplement your dog's food with fresh garlic (minced or grated) and an hearty amount of brewer's yeast, both of which ward off fleas.
- Use a flea comb on your dog daily. Submerge fleas in a cup of bleach to kill them quickly.
- Confine the dog to only a few rooms to limit the spread of fleas in the home.
- Vacuum daily...and get all of the crevices! Dispose of the bag every few days until the problem is under control.
- Wash your dog's bedding daily. Cover cushions where your dog sleeps with towels, and wash the towels often.

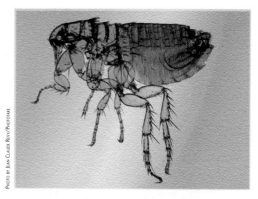

PHOTO BY JEAN CLAUDE REVY/PHOTOTAKE

A LOOK AT FLEAS

Fleas have been around for millions of years and have adapted to changing host animals. They are able to go through a complete life cycle in less than one month or they can extend their lives to almost two years by remaining as pupae or cocoons. They do not need blood or any other food for up to 20 months.

They have been measured as being able to jump 300,000 times and can jump 150 times their length in any direction, including straight up. Those are just a few of the reasons why they are so successful in infesting a dog!

THE LIFE CYCLE OF THE FLEA

Photos courtesy of Fleabusters' Rx for Fleas.

Egg

Larva

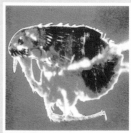

Pupa

Adult

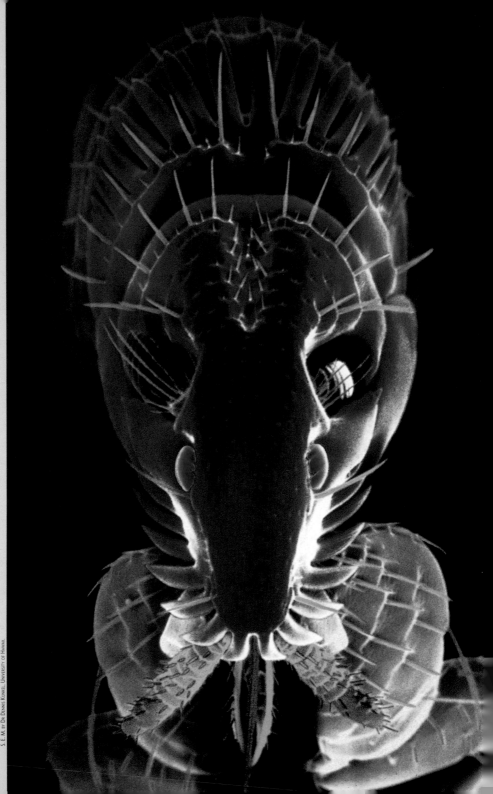

A scanning electron micrograph of a dog or cat flea, *Ctenocephalides,* magnified more than 100x. This image has been colorized for effect.

be in the form of a collar or a spray, but more recent innovations include digestible insecticides that poison the fleas when they ingest the dog's blood. Alternatively, there are drops that, when placed on the back of the dog's neck, spread throughout the hair and skin to kill adult fleas.

INSECT GROWTH REGULATOR (IGR)

Two types of products should be used when treating fleas—a product to treat the pet and a product to treat the home. Adult fleas represent less than 1% of the flea population. The pre-adult fleas (eggs, larvae and pupae) represent more than 99% of the flea population and are found in the environment; it is in the case of pre-adult fleas that products containing an Insect Growth Regulator (IGR) should be used in the home.

IGRs are a new class of compounds used to prevent the development of insects. They do not kill the insect outright, but instead use the insect's biology against it to stop it from completing its growth. Products that contain methoprene are the world's first and leading IGRs. Used to control fleas and other insects, this type of IGR will stop flea larvae from developing and protect the house for up to seven months.

DO NOT MIX

Never mix flea-control products without first consulting your vet. Some products can become toxic when combined with others and can cause fatal consequences.

TICKS AND MITES

Though not as common as fleas, ticks and mites are found all over the tropical and temperate world. They don't bite, like fleas; they harpoon. They dig their sharp proboscis (nose) into the dog's skin and drink the blood. Their only food and drink is dog's blood. Dogs can get Lyme disease, Rocky Mountain spotted fever (normally found in the US only), tick bite paralysis and many other diseases from ticks and mites. They may live where fleas are found and they like to hide in cracks or seams in walls. They are controlled the same way fleas are controlled.

The dog tick, *Dermacentor variabilis*, may well be the most common dog tick in many geographical areas, especially those areas where the climate is hot and humid. Most dog ticks have life

A brown dog tick, *Rhipicephalus sanguineus*, is an uncommon but annoying tick found on dogs.

The head of a dog tick, *Dermacentor variabilis*, enlarged and colorized for effect.

PHOTO BY DR DENNIS KUNKEL, UNIVERSITY OF HAWAII

The great outdoors may be fun for your dog, but it also is an home to dangerous ticks. Deer ticks carry a bacterium known as *Borrelia burgdorferi* and are most active in the autumn and spring. When infections are caught early, penicillin and tetracycline are effective antibiotics, but if left untreated the bacteria may cause neurological, kidney and cardiac problems as well as long-term trouble with walking and painful joints.

S. E. M. BY DR ANDREW SPIELMAN/PHOTOTAKE

expectancies of a week to six months, depending upon climatic conditions. They can neither jump nor fly, but they can crawl slowly and can range up to 5 metres (16 feet) to reach a sleeping or unsuspecting dog.

Human lice look like dog lice; the two are closely related.

PHOTO BY DWIGHT R KUHN

MANGE

Mites cause a skin irritation called mange. Some mites are contagious, like *Cheyletiella*, ear mites, scabies and chiggers. Mites that infest ears are usually controlled with Lindane, which can

only be administered by a vet, followed by Tresaderm at home. It is essential that your dog be treated for mange as quickly as possible because some forms of mange are transmissible to people.

Opposite page:
The dog tick, *Dermacentor variabilis*, is probably the most common tick found on dogs. Look at the strength in its eight legs! No wonder it's hard to detach them.

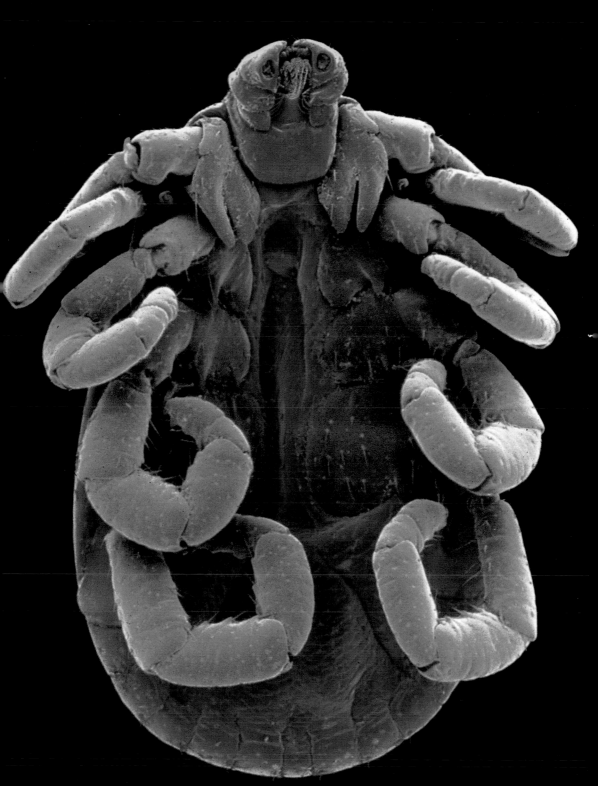

The mange mite, Psoroptes bovis.

INTERNAL PARASITES

Most animals—fishes, birds and mammals, including dogs and humans—have worms and other parasites that live inside their bodies. According to Dr Herbert R Axelrod, the fish pathologist, there are two kinds of parasites: dumb and smart. The smart parasites live in peaceful cooperation with their hosts (symbiosis), while the dumb parasites kill their hosts. Most worm infections are relatively easy to control. If they are not controlled, they weaken the host dog to the point that other medical problems occur, but they do not kill the host as dumb parasites would.

ROUNDWORMS

The roundworms that infect dogs are known scientifically as *Toxocara canis*. They live in the dog's intestines and shed eggs continually. It has been estimated that a dog produces about 150 grammes of faeces every day. Each gramme of faeces averages 10,000–12,000 eggs of round-worms. There are no known areas in which dogs roam that do not contain roundworm eggs. The greatest danger of roundworms is

ROUNDWORMS

Average-size dogs can pass 1,360,000 roundworm eggs every day. For example, if there were only 1 million dogs in the world, the world would be saturated with 1,300 metric tonnes of dog faeces. These faeces would contain 15,000,000,000 roundworm eggs.

Up to 31% of home gardens and children's play boxes in the US contain roundworm eggs.

Flushing dog's faeces down the toilet is not a safe practice because the usual sewage treatments do not destroy roundworm eggs.

Infected puppies start shedding roundworm eggs at three weeks of age. They can be infected by their mother's milk.

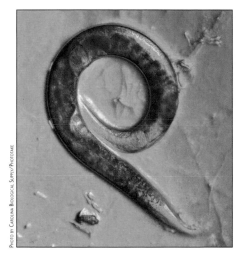

The roundworm *Rhabditis* can infect both dogs and humans.

that they infect people too! It is wise to have your dog tested regularly for roundworms.

Pigs also have roundworm infections that can be passed to humans and dogs. The typical roundworm parasite is called *Ascaris lumbricoides*.

DEWORMING

Ridding your puppy of worms is *very important* because certain worms that puppies carry, such as tapeworms and roundworms, can infect humans.

Breeders initiate deworming programmes at or about four weeks of age. The routine is repeated every two or three weeks until the puppy is three months old. The breeder from whom you obtained your puppy should provide you with the complete details of the deworming programme.

Your veterinary surgeon can prescribe and monitor the programme of deworming for you. The usual programme is treating the puppy every 15–20 days until the puppy is positively worm-free. It is advised that you only treat your puppy with drugs that are recommended professionally.

The common roundworm, *Ascaris lumbricoides*.

Left: *Ancylostoma caninum* is uncommonly found in pet or show dogs in Britain.

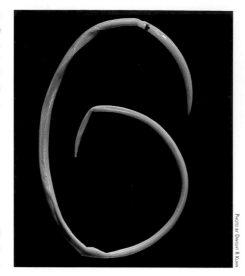

Right: Male and female hookworms.

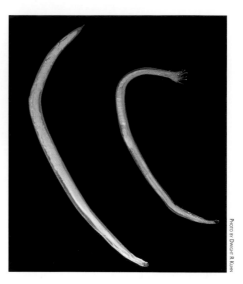

PHOTO BY DWIGHT R KUHN

PHOTO BY DWIGHT R KUHN

HOOKWORMS

The worm *Ancylostoma caninum* is commonly called the dog hookworm. It is also dangerous to humans and cats. It has teeth by which it attaches itself to the intestines of the dog. It changes the site of its attachment about six times a day and the dog loses blood from each detachment, possibly causing iron-deficiency anaemia. Hookworms are easily purged from the dog with many medications. Milbemycin oxime, which also serves as an heartworm preventative in

The infective stage of the hookworm larva.

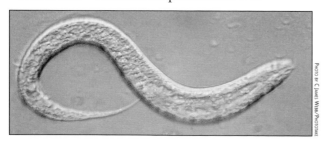

PHOTO BY C JAMES WEBB/PHOTOTAKE

Collies, can be used for this purpose.

In Britain, the 'temperate climate' hookworm (*Uncinaria stenocephala*) is rarely found in pet or show dogs, but can occur in hunting packs, racing Greyhounds and sheepdogs because the worms can be prevalent wherever dogs are exercised regularly on grassland.

TAPEWORMS

There are many species of tapeworm, all of which are carried by fleas! The dog eats the flea and starts the tapeworm cycle. Humans can also be infected with tapeworms—so don't eat fleas! Fleas are so small that your dog could pass them onto your hands, your plate or your food and thus make it possible for you to ingest a flea that is carrying tapeworm eggs.

TAPEWORMS

Humans, rats, squirrels, foxes, coyotes, wolves and domestic dogs are all susceptible to tapeworm infection. Except in humans, tapeworms are usually not a fatal infection. Infected individuals can harbour 1000 parasitic worms.

Tapeworms, like some other types of worm, are hermaphroditic, meaning male and female in the same worm.

If dogs eat infected rats or mice, or anything carrying tapeworm, they get the tapeworm disease. One month after attaching to a dog's intestine, the worm starts shedding eggs. These eggs are infective immediately. Infective eggs can live for a few months without an host animal.

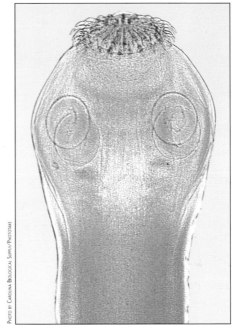

The head and rostellum (the round prominence on the scolex) of a tapeworm, which infects dogs and humans.

While tapeworm infection is not life-threatening in dogs (smart parasite!), it can be the cause of a very serious liver disease for humans. About 50% of the humans infected with *Echinococcus multilocularis*, a type of tapeworm that causes alveolar hydatis, perish.

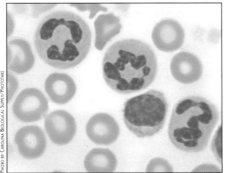

Magnified heartworm larvae, *Dirofilaria immitis*.

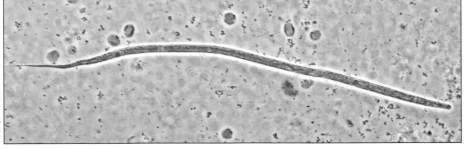

Heartworm, *Dirofilaria immitis*.

First Aid at a Glance

Burns
Place the affected area under cool water; use ice if only a small area is burnt.

Insect bites
Apply ice to relieve swelling; antihistamine dosed properly.

Animal bites
Clean any bleeding area; apply pressure until bleeding subsides; go to the vet.

Spider bites
Use cold compress and a pressurised pack to inhibit venom's spreading.

Antifreeze poisoning
Induce vomiting with hydrogen peroxide. Seek *immediate* veterinary help!

Fish hooks
Removal best handled by vet; hook must be cut in order to remove.

Snake bites
Pack ice around bite; contact vet quickly; identify snake for proper antivenin.

Road-traffic accident
Move dog from roadway with blanket; seek veterinary aid.

Shock
Calm the dog, keep him warm; seek immediate veterinary help.

Nosebleed
Apply cold compress to the nose; apply pressure to any visible abrasion.

Bleeding
Apply pressure above the area; treat wound by applying a cotton pack.

Heat stroke
Submerge dog in cold bath; cool down with fresh air and water; go to the vet.

Frostbite/Hypothermia
Warm the dog with a warm bath, electric blankets or hot water bottles.

Abrasions
Clean the wound and wash out thoroughly with fresh water; apply antiseptic.

 Remember: an injured dog may attempt to bite an helping hand from fear and confusion. Always muzzle the dog before trying to offer assistance.

HEARTWORMS

Heartworms are thin, extended worms up to 30 cms (12 ins) long, which live in a dog's heart and the major blood vessels surrounding it. Dogs may have up to 200 worms. Symptoms may be loss of energy, loss of appetite, coughing, the development of a pot belly and anaemia.

Heartworms are transmitted by mosquitoes. The mosquito drinks the blood of an infected dog and takes in larvae with the blood. The larvae, called microfilariae, develop within the body of the mosquito and are passed on to the next dog bitten after the larvae mature. It takes two to three weeks for the larvae to develop to the infective stage within the body of the mosquito. Dogs are usually treated at about six weeks of age, and maintained on a prophylactic dose given monthly.

Blood testing for heartworms is not necessarily indicative of how seriously your dog is infected. This is a dangerous disease. Although heartworm is a problem for dogs in America, Australia, Asia and Central Europe, dogs in the United Kingdom currently are not affected by heartworm.

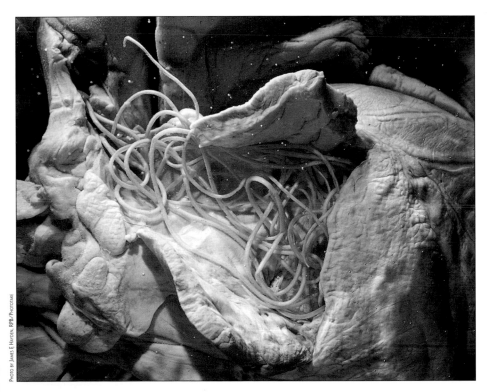

The heart of a dog infected with canine heartworm, *Dirofilaria immitis.*

HOMEOPATHY:
an alternative to conventional medicine

'Less Is Most'

Using this principle, the strength of an homeopathic remedy is measured by the number of serial dilutions that were undertaken to create it. The greater the number of serial dilutions, the greater the strength of the homeopathic remedy. The potency of a remedy that has been made by making a dilution of 1 part in 100 parts (or 1/100) is 1c or 1cH. If this remedy is subjected to a series of further dilutions, each one being 1/100, a more dilute and stronger remedy is produced. If the remedy is diluted in this way six times, it is called 6c or 6cH. A dilution of 6c is 1 part in 1,000,000,000,000. In general, higher potencies in more frequent doses are better for acute symptoms and lower potencies in more infrequent doses are more useful for chronic, long-standing problems.

CURING OUR DOGS NATURALLY

Holistic medicine means treating the whole animal as a unique, perfect living being. Generally, holistic treatments do not suppress the symptoms that the body naturally produces, as do most medications prescribed by conventional doctors and vets. Holistic methods seek to cure disease by regaining balance and harmony in the patient's environment. Some of these methods include use of nutritional therapy, herbs, flower essences, aromatherapy, acupuncture, massage, chiropractic and, of course, the most popular holistic approach, homeopathy.

Homeopathy is a theory or system of treating illness with small doses of substances which, if administered in larger quantities, would produce the symptoms that the patient already has. This approach is often described as 'like cures like.' Although modern veterinary medicine is geared toward the 'quick fix,' homeopathy relies on the belief that, given the time, the body is able to heal itself and return to its natural, healthy state.

Choosing a remedy to cure a problem in our dogs is the difficult part of homeopathy. Consult with your veterinary surgeon for a professional diagnosis of your dog's symptoms. Often these symptoms require immediate conventional care. If your vet is willing, and knowledgeable, you may attempt an homeopathic remedy. Be aware that cortisone prevents homeopathic remedies from working. There are hundreds of possibilities and combinations to cure many problems in dogs, from basic physical problems such as excessive moulting, fleas or other parasites, unattractive doggy odour, bad breath, upset tummy, obesity,

dry, oily or dull coat, diarrhoea, ear problems or eye discharge (including tears and dry or mucousy matter), to behavioural abnormalities such as fear of loud noises, habitual licking, poor appetite, excessive barking and various phobias. From alumina to zincum metallicum, the remedies span the planet and the imagination…from flowers and weeds to chemicals, insect droppings, diesel smoke and volcanic ash.

Using 'Like to Treat Like'

Unlike conventional medicines that suppress symptoms, homeopathic remedies treat illnesses with small doses of substances that, if administered in larger quantities, would produce the symptoms that the patient already has. While the same homeopathic remedy can be used to treat different symptoms in different dogs, here are some interesting remedies and their uses.

Apis Mellifica
(made from honey bee venom) can be used for allergies or to reduce swelling that occurs in acutely infected kidneys.

Diesel Smoke
can be used to help control travel sickness.

Calcarea Fluorica
(made from calcium fluoride, which helps harden bone structure) can be useful in treating hard lumps in tissues.

Natrum Muriaticum
(made from common salt, sodium chloride) is useful in treating thin, thirsty dogs.

Nitricum Acidum
(made from nitric acid) is used for symptoms you would expect to see from contact with acids, such as lesions, especially where the skin joins the linings of body orifices or openings such as the lips and nostrils.

Symphytum
(made from the herb Knitbone, *Symphytum officianale*) is used to encourage bones to heal.

Urtica Urens
(made from the common stinging nettle) is used in treating painful, irritating rashes.

HOMEOPATHIC REMEDIES FOR YOUR DOG

Symptom/Ailment	Possible Remedy
ALLERGIES	Apis Mellifica 30c, Astacus Fluviatilis 6c, Pulsatilla 30c, Urtica Urens 6c
ALOPAECIA	Alumina 30c, Lycopodium 30c, Sepia 30c, Thallium 6c
ANAL GLANDS (BLOCKED)	Hepar Sulphuris Calcareum 30c, Sanicula 6c, Silicea 6c
ARTHRITIS	Rhus Toxicodendron 6c, Bryonia Alba 6c
CATARACT	Calcarea Carbonica 6c, Conium Maculatum 6c, Phosphorus 30c, Silicea 30c
CONSTIPATION	Alumina 6c, Carbo Vegetabilis 30c, Graphites 6c, Nitricum Acidum 30c, Silicea 6c
COUGHING	Aconitum Napellus 6c, Belladonna 30c, Hyoscyamus Niger 30c, Phosphorus 30c
DIARRHOEA	Arsenicum Album 30c, Aconitum Napellus 6c, Chamomilla 30c, Mercurius Corrosivus 30c
DRY EYE	Zincum Metallicum 30c
EAR PROBLEMS	Aconitum Napellus 30c, Belladonna 30c, Hepar Sulphuris 30c, Tellurium 30c, Psorinum 200c
EYE PROBLEMS	Borax 6c, Aconitum Napellus 30c, Graphites 6c, Staphysagria 6c, Thuja Occidentalis 30c
GLAUCOMA	Aconitum Napellus 30c, Apis Mellifica 6c, Phosphorus 30c
HEAT STROKE	Belladonna 30c, Gelsemium Sempervirens 30c, Sulphur 30c
HICCOUGHS	Cinchona Deficinalis 6c
HIP DYSPLASIA	Colocynthis 6c, Rhus Toxicodendron 6c, Bryonia Alba 6c
INCONTINENCE	Argentum Nitricum 6c, Causticum 30c, Conium Maculatum 30c, Pulsatilla 30c, Sepia 30c
INSECT BITES	Apis Mellifica 30c, Cantharis 30c, Hypericum Perforatum 6c, Urtica Urens 30c
ITCHING	Alumina 30c, Arsenicum Album 30c, Carbo Vegetabilis 30c, Hypericum Perforatum 6c, Mezerium 6c, Sulphur 30c
KENNEL COUGH	Drosera 6c, Ipecacuanha 30c
MASTITIS	Apis Mellifica 30c, Belladonna 30c, Urtica Urens 1m
PATELLAR LUXATION	Gelsemium Sempervirens 6c, Rhus Toxicodendron 6c
PENIS PROBLEMS	Aconitum Napellus 30c, Hepar Sulphuris Calcareum 30c, Pulsatilla 30c, Thuja Occidentalis 6c
PUPPY TEETHING	Calcarea Carbonica 6c, Chamomilla 6c, Phytolacca 6c
TRAVEL SICKNESS	Cocculus 6c, Petroleum 6c

Recognising a Sick Dog

Unlike colicky babies and cranky children, our canine charges cannot tell us when they are feeling ill. Therefore, there are a number of signs that owners can identify to know that their dogs are not feeling well.

Take note for physical manifestations such as:

- unusual, bad odour, including bad breath
- excessive moulting
- wax in the ears, chronic ear irritation
- oily, flaky, dull haircoat
- mucous, tearing or similar discharge in the eyes
- fleas or mites
- mucous in stool, diarrhoea
- sensitivity to petting or handling
- licking at paws, scratching face, etc.

Keep an eye out for behavioural changes as well including:

- lethargy, idleness
- lack of patience or general irritability
- lack of appetite
- phobias (fear of people, loud noises, etc.)
- strange behaviour, suspicion, fear
- coprophagia
- more frequent barking
- whimpering, crying

Get Well Soon

You don't need a DVR or a BVMA to provide good TLC to your sick or recovering dog, but you do need to pay attention to some details that normally wouldn't bother him. The following tips will aid Fido's recovery and get him back on his paws again:

- Keep his space free of irritating smells, like heavy perfumes and air fresheners.
- Rest is the best medicine! Avoid harsh lighting that will prevent your dog from sleeping. Shade him from bright sunlight during the day and dim the lights in the evening.
- Keep the noise level down. Animals are more sensitive to sound when they are sick.

- Be attentive to any necessary temperature adjustments. A dog with a fever needs a cool room and cold liquids. A bitch that is whelping or recovering from surgery will be more comfortable in a warm room, consuming warm liquids and food.
- You wouldn't send a sick child back to school early, so don't rush your dog back into a full routine until he seems absolutely ready.

Number-One Killer Disease in Dogs: CANCER

In every age, there is a word associated with a disease or plague that causes humans to shudder. In the 21st century, that word is 'cancer.' Just as cancer is the leading cause of death in humans, it claims nearly half the lives of dogs that die from a natural disease as well as half the dogs that die over the age of ten years.

Described as a genetic disease, cancer becomes a greater risk as the dog ages. Veterinary surgeons and dog owners have become increasingly aware of the threat of cancer to dogs. Statistics reveal that one dog in every five will develop cancer, the most common of which is skin cancer. Many cancers, including prostate, ovarian and breast cancer, can be avoided by spaying and neutering our dogs by the age of six months.

Early detection of cancer can save or extend your dog's life, so it is absolutely vital for owners to have their dogs examined by a qualified veterinary surgeon or oncologist immediately upon detection of any abnormality. Certain dietary guidelines have also proven to reduce the onset and spread of cancer. Foods based on fish rather than beef, due to the presence of Omega-3 fatty acids, are recommended. Other amino acids such as glutamine have significant benefits for canines, particularly those breeds that show a greater susceptibility to cancer.

Cancer management and treatments promise hope for future generations of canines. Since the disease is genetic, breeders should never breed a dog whose parents, grandparents and any related siblings have developed cancer. It is difficult to know whether to exclude an otherwise healthy dog from a breeding programme as the disease does not manifest itself until the dog's senior years.

RECOGNISE CANCER WARNING SIGNS

Since early detection can possibly rescue your dog from becoming a cancer statistic, it is essential for owners to recognise the possible signs and seek the assistance of a qualified professional.

- Abnormal bumps or lumps that continue to grow
- Bleeding or discharge from any body cavity
- Persistent stiffness or lameness
- Recurrent sores or sores that do not heal
- Inappetence
- Breathing difficulties
- Weight loss
- Bad breath or odours
- General malaise and fatigue
- Eating and swallowing problems
- Difficulty urinating and defecating

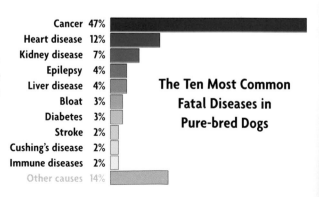

Cancer	47%
Heart disease	12%
Kidney disease	7%
Epilepsy	4%
Liver disease	4%
Bloat	3%
Diabetes	3%
Stroke	2%
Cushing's disease	2%
Immune diseases	2%
Other causes	14%

The Ten Most Common Fatal Diseases in Pure-bred Dogs

CDS: COGNITIVE DYSFUNCTION SYNDROME
'OLD-DOG SYNDROME'

There are many ways for you to evaluate old-dog syndrome. Veterinary surgeons have defined CDS (cognitive dysfunction syndrome) as the gradual deterioration of cognitive abilities. These are indicated by changes in the dog's behaviour. When a dog changes his routine response, and maladies have been eliminated as the cause of these behavioural changes, then CDS is the usual diagnosis.

More than half the dogs over 8 years old suffer from some form of CDS. The older the dog, the more chance it has of suffering from CDS. In humans, doctors often dismiss the CDS behavioural changes as part of 'winding down.'

There are four major signs of CDS: frequent toilet accidents inside the home, sleeping much more or much less than normal, acting confused and failing to respond to social stimuli.

SYMPTOMS OF CDS

FREQUENT TOILET ACCIDENTS
- Urinates in the house.
- Defecates in the house.
- Doesn't signal that he wants to go out.

SLEEP PATTERNS
- Moves much more slowly.
- Sleeps more than normal during the day.
- Sleeps less during the night.

CONFUSION
- Goes outside and just stands there.
- Appears confused with a faraway look in his eyes.
- Hides more often.
- Doesn't recognise friends.
- Doesn't come when called.
- Walks around listlessly and without a destination.

FAILURE TO RESPOND TO SOCIAL STIMULI
- Comes to people less frequently, whether called or not.
- Doesn't tolerate petting for more than a short time.
- Doesn't come to the door when you return home.

The term 'old' is a qualitative term. For dogs, as well as for their masters, old is relative. If people live to be 100 years old, dogs live to be 20 years old. While this might seem like a good rule of thumb, it is very inaccurate. When trying to compare dog years to human years, you cannot make a generalisation about all dogs. You can make the generalisation that Sussex Spaniels have a lifespan of 12 years on the average, with the typical range being between 11 and 15 years.

The Sussex is considered physically mature at about three years of age, but can reproduce even earlier. So, again to generalise, the first three years of a dog's life are like seven times that of a comparable human. That means a 3-year-old dog is like a 21-year-old human. However, as the curve of comparison shows, there is no hard and fast rule for comparing dog and human age. Small breeds tend to live longer than large breeds, some breeds' adolescent periods last longer than others' and some breeds experience rapid periods of growth. The comparison is made even more difficult, for,

likewise, not all humans age at the same rate...and human females live longer than human males.

WHAT TO LOOK FOR IN VETERANS

The typical age at which a dog is considered a 'veteran' or 'senior' can vary according to breed. It is probably safe to say that by age 11 years, most Sussex Spaniels are retired or semi-retired from strenuous physical activities, though most appreciate being included in shorter and less strenuous sessions of regular activities such as hunting. Keeping a Sussex Spaniel active as befits his age is recommended for both mental and physical well-being.

In terms of veterinary care, most veterinary surgeons and behaviourists use the seven-year mark as the time to consider a dog a 'senior' or 'veteran.' Neither term implies that the dog is geriatric and has begun to fail in mind and body. Ageing is essentially a slowing process. Humans readily admit that they feel a difference in their activity level from age 20 to 30, and then from 30 to 40, etc. By treating the seven-year-old dog as a veteran, owners are able to implement certain therapeutic and preventative medical strategies with the help of their veterinary surgeons.

A special-care programme should include at least two veterinary visits per year and screening sessions to determine the dog's health status, as well as nutritional counselling. Veterinary surgeons determine the senior dog's health status through a blood smear for a complete blood count, serum chemistry profile with electrolytes, urinalysis, blood pressure check, electrocardiogram, ocular tonometry (pressure on the eyeball) and dental prophylaxis.

Such an extensive programme for senior dogs is well advised before owners start to see the obvious physical signs of ageing, such as slower and inhibited movement, greying, increased sleep/nap periods and disinterest in play and other activity. This preventative programme promises a longer, healthier life for the ageing dog. Among the physical problems common in ageing dogs are the loss of sight and hearing, arthritis, kidney and liver failure, diabetes mellitus, heart disease and Cushing's disease (an hormonal disease).

In addition to the physical manifestations discussed, there are some behavioural changes and problems related to ageing dogs. Dogs suffering from hearing or vision loss, dental discomfort or arthritis can become aggressive. Likewise, the near-deaf and/or blind dog may be startled more easily and react in an unexpectedly aggressive manner. Veterans suffering from senility can become more impatient and irritable. Housesoiling accidents are associated with loss of mobility, kidney problems and loss of sphincter control as well as plaque accumulation, physiological brain changes and reactions to medications. Older dogs, just like young puppies, suffer from separation anxiety, which can lead to excessive barking, whining, housesoiling and destructive behaviour. Veterans may become fearful of everyday sounds, such as vacuum cleaners, heaters, thunder

A veteran Sussex, still alert, in great condition and 'sitting pretty.'

and passing traffic. Some dogs have difficulty sleeping, due to discomfort, the need for frequent toilet visits and the like.

Owners should avoid spoiling the older dog with too many fatty treats. Obesity is a common problem in older dogs and subtracts years from their lives. Keep the senior dog as trim as possible, since excessive weight puts additional stress on the body's vital organs. Some breeders recommend supplementing the diet with foods high in fibre and lower in calories. Adding fresh vegetables and marrow broth to the veteran's diet makes a tasty, low-calorie, low-fat supplement. Vets also offer speciality diets for senior dogs that are worth exploring.

Your dog, as he nears his twilight years, needs your patience and good care more than ever. Never punish an older dog for an accident or abnormal behaviour. For all the years of love, protection and companionship that your dog has provided, he deserves special attention and courtesies. The older dog may need to relieve himself at 3 a.m. because he can no longer hold it for eight hours. Older dogs may not be able to remain crated for more than two or three hours. It may be time to give up a sofa or chair to your old friend. Although he may not seem as enthusiastic about your attention and petting, he does appreciate the considerations you offer as he gets older.

Your Sussex Spaniel does not understand why his world is slowing down. Owners must make their dogs' transition into their golden years as pleasant and rewarding as possible.

WHAT TO DO WHEN THE TIME COMES

You are never fully prepared to make a rational decision about putting your dog to sleep. It is very obvious that you love your Sussex Spaniel or you would not be reading this book. Putting a beloved dog to sleep is extremely difficult. It is a decision that must be made with your veterinary surgeon. You are usually forced to make the decision when your dog experiences one or more life-threatening symptoms that have become serious enough for you to seek veterinary help.

If the prognosis of the malady indicates that the end is near and that your beloved pet will only continue to suffer and experience no enjoyment for the balance of his life, then euthanasia is the right choice.

WHAT IS EUTHANASIA?

Euthanasia derives from the Greek, meaning 'good death.' In other words, it means the planned, painless killing of a dog suffering from a painful, incurable condition, or who is so aged that he cannot walk, see, eat or control his excretory functions. Euthanasia is usually accomplished by injection with an overdose of anaesthesia or a barbiturate. Aside from the prick of the needle, the experience is usually painless.

MAKING THE DECISION

The decision to euthanise your dog is never easy. The days during which the dog becomes ill and the end occurs can be unusually stressful for you. If this is your first experience with the death of a loved one, you may need the comfort dictated by your religious beliefs. If you are the head of the family and have children, you should have involved them in the decision of putting your Sussex Spaniel to sleep. Usually your dog can be maintained on drugs for a few days in order to give you ample time to make a decision. During this time, talking with members of your family or with people who have lived through the same experience can ease the burden of your inevitable decision.

THE FINAL RESTING PLACE

Dogs can have some of the same privileges as humans. The remains of your beloved dog can be buried in a pet cemetery, which is generally expensive. Alternatively, your dog can be cremated individually and the ashes returned to you. A less expensive option is mass cremation, although, of course, the ashes cannot then be returned. Vets can usually arrange the cremation on your behalf. The cost of these options should always be discussed frankly and openly with your veterinary surgeon. In Britain, if your dog has died at the surgery, the vet legally cannot allow you to take your dog's body home, as home garden burials are not permitted.

GETTING ANOTHER DOG?

The grief of losing your beloved dog will be as lasting as the grief of losing an human friend or relative. In most cases, if your dog died of old age (if there is such a thing), it had slowed down considerably. Do you want a new Sussex Spaniel puppy to replace it? Or are you better off finding a more mature Sussex Spaniel, say two to three years of age, which will usually be house-trained and will have an already developed personality. In this case, you can find out if you like each other after a few hours of being together.

The decision is, of course, your own. Do you want another Sussex Spaniel or perhaps a different breed so as to avoid comparison with your beloved friend? Most people usually buy the same breed because they know (and love) the characteristics of that breed. Then, too, they often know people who have the same breed and perhaps they are lucky enough that one of their friends expects a litter soon. What could be better?

SHOWING YOUR
SUSSEX SPANIEL

SHOW RING ETIQUETTE

Just as with anything else, there is a certain etiquette to the show ring that can only be learned through experience. Showing your dog can be quite intimidating to you as a novice when it seems as if everyone else knows what he is doing. You can familiarise yourself with ring procedure beforehand by taking ringcraft classes to prepare you and your dog for conformation showing and by talking with experienced handlers. When you are in the ring, it is very important to pay attention and listen to the instructions you are given about where to move your dog. Remember, even the most skilled handlers had to start somewhere. Keep it up and you too will become a proficient handler as you gain practice and experience.

When you purchase your Sussex Spaniel, you will make it clear to the breeder whether you want one just as a loveable companion and pet, or if you hope to be buying a Sussex with show prospects. No reputable breeder will sell you a young puppy and tell you that it is *definitely* of show quality, for so much can go wrong during the early months of a puppy's development. If you plan to show, what you will hopefully have acquired is a puppy with 'show potential.'

To the novice, exhibiting a Sussex Spaniel in the show ring may look easy, but it takes a lot of hard work and devotion to do top winning at a show such as the prestigious Crufts Dog Show, not to mention a little luck too!

The first concept that the canine novice learns when watching a dog show is that each dog first competes against members of his own breed. Once the judge has selected the best member of each breed (Best of Breed), provided that the show is judged on a Group system, that chosen dog will compete with other dogs in his group. Finally, the best of each group will compete for Best in Show.

The second concept that you must understand is that the dogs are not actually compared against one another. The judge compares each dog against his breed standard, which is the written description of the ideal specimen of the breed. While some early breed standards were indeed based on specific dogs that were famous or popular, many dedicated enthusiasts say that a perfect specimen, as described in the standard, has never walked into a show ring, has never been bred and, to the woe of dog breeders around the globe, does not exist. Breeders attempt to get as close to this ideal as possible with every litter, but theoretically the 'perfect' dog is so elusive that it is impossible. (And if the 'perfect' dog were born, breeders and judges probably would never agree that it was indeed 'perfect.')

If you are interested in exploring the world of dog showing, your best bet is to join your local breed club. These clubs often host both Championship and Open Shows, and sometimes Match meetings and special events, all of which could be of interest, even if you are only an onlooker. Clubs also send out newsletters, and some organise training days and seminars in order that people may learn more about their chosen breed.

INFORMATION ON CLUBS

You can get information about dog shows from national kennel clubs:

The Kennel Club
1-5 Clarges St., Piccadilly, London W1Y 8AB
UK
www.the-kennel-club.org.uk

Fédération Cynologique Internationale
14, rue Leopold II, B-6530 Thuin, Belgium
www.fci.be

American Kennel Club
5580 Centerview Dr., Raleigh, NC 27606-3390
USA
www.akc.org

Canadian Kennel Club
89 Skyway Ave., Suite 100, Etobicoke, Ontario
M9W 6R4 Canada
www.ckc.ca

At benched shows, dogs wait in designated areas, usually grouped by breed, until their time in the ring.

benched show in England. Every year over 20,000 of the UK's best dogs qualify to participate in this marvellous show, which lasts four days.

The Kennel Club governs many different kinds of shows in Great Britain, Australia, South Africa and beyond. At the most competitive and prestigious of these shows, the Championship Shows, a dog can earn Challenge Certificates (CCs), and thereby become a Show Champion or a Champion. A dog must earn three CCs under three different judges to earn the prefix of 'Sh Ch' or 'Ch.' Some breeds must also qualify in a field trial in order to gain the title of full Champion, and the Sussex Spaniel is one such breed. CCs are awarded to a very small percentage of the dogs competing, and dogs that are already Champions compete with others for these coveted CCs. The

To locate the breed club closest to you, contact The Kennel Club, the ruling body for the British dog world. The Kennel Club governs not only conformation shows but also working trials, obedience shows, agility trials, field trials, etc. The Kennel Club furnishes the rules and regulations for all of these events plus general dog registration and other basic requirements of dog ownership. Its annual show, called the Crufts Dog Show, held in Birmingham, is the largest

TIDINESS COUNTS

Surely you've spent hours grooming your dog to perfection for the show ring, but don't forget about yourself! While the dog should be the centre of attention, it is important that you also appear clean and tidy. Wear smart, appropriate clothes and comfortable shoes in a colour that contrasts with your dog's coat. Look and act like a professional.

THE TITLE OF CHAMPION

Until 1950, a dog in Britain could earn the title of Champion by winning three Challenge Certificates or tickets. Today, the prestigious title of Champion requires that the dog win three tickets and qualify in the field. The Kennel Club introduced the title of Show Champion for the dog winning three tickets (but without a field qualification). A Dual Champion is a dog that has obtained the title of Show Champion as well as that of Field Trial Champion.

Open Shows are generally less competitive and are frequently used as 'practice shows' for young dogs. There are hundreds of Open Shows each year that can be delightful social events and are great first show experiences for the novice. Even if you're considering just watching a show to wet your paws, an Open Show is a great choice.

While Championship and Open Shows are most important for the beginner to understand, there are other types of shows in which the interested dog owner can participate. Training clubs sponsor Matches that can be

number of CCs awarded in any one year is based upon the total number of dogs in each breed entered for competition.

There are three types of Championship Shows: an all-breed General Championship Show for all Kennel-Club-recognised breeds; a Group Championship Show, which is limited to breeds within one of the groups; and a Breed Show, which is usually confined to a single breed. The Kennel Club determines which breeds at which Championship Shows will have the opportunity to earn CCs (or tickets). Serious exhibitors often will opt not to participate if the tickets are withheld at a particular show. This policy makes earning championships even more difficult to accomplish.

The Best of Breed Sussex Spaniel at the prestigious Crufts Dog Show in 2000.

The judge assesses the line of Sussex in the breed ring, not comparing the dogs against each other, but rather deciding which of the competitors most closely matches the ideal set forth in the breed standard.

entered on the day of the show for a nominal fee. In these introductory-level exhibitions, two dogs' names are pulled out of an hat and 'matched,' the winner of that match goes on to the next round and eventually only one dog is left undefeated.

Exemption Shows are much more light-hearted affairs with usually only four pedigree classes and several 'fun' classes, all of which can be entered on the day of the show. Exemption Shows are sometimes held in conjunction with small agricultural shows and the proceeds must be given to a charity. Limited Shows are also available in small number. Entry is restricted to members of the club that hosts the show, although you can usually join the club when making an entry.

Before you actually step into the ring, you would be well advised to sit back and observe the judge's ring procedure. If it is your first time in the ring, do not be over-anxious and run to the front of the line. It is much better to stand back and study how the exhibitor in front of you is performing. The judge asks each handler to 'stand' the dog, hopefully showing the dog off to his best advantage. The judge will observe the dog from a distance and from different angles, and approach the dog to check his teeth, overall structure, alertness and muscle tone, as well as consider how well the dog 'conforms' to the standard. Most importantly, the judge will have the exhibitor move the dog around the ring in some pattern that he or she should specify (another advantage to not going first, but always listen since some judges change their directions—and the judge is *always* right!).

A GENTLEMAN'S SPORT

Whether or not your dog wins top honours, showing is a pleasant social event. Sometimes, one may meet a troublemaker or nasty exhibitor, but these people should be ignored and forgotten. In the extremely rare case that someone threatens or harasses you or your dog, you can lodge a complaint with The Kennel Club. This should be done with extreme prudence. Complaints are investigated seriously and should never be filed on a whim.

Finally, the judge will give the dog one last look before moving on to the next exhibitor.

If you are not in the top three at your first show, do not be discouraged. Be patient and consistent, and you may eventually find yourself in the winning line-up. Remember that the winners were once in your shoes and have devoted many hours and much money to earn the placement. If you find that your dog is losing every time and never getting a nod, it may be time to consider a different dog sport or to just enjoy your Sussex Spaniel as a pet.

Virtually all countries with a recognised speciality breed club (sometimes called a 'parent' club) offer show conformation competition specifically for and among Sussex Spaniels. Under direction of the club, other special events for hunting, tracking, obedience and agility may be offered as well, whether for titling or just for fun.

WORKING TRIALS

Working trials can be entered by any well-trained dog of any breed, not just Gundogs or Working dogs. Many dogs that earn the Kennel Club Good Citizen Dog award choose to participate in a working trial. There are five stakes at both Open and Championship levels: Companion Dog (CD), Utility Dog (UD), Working Dog (WD), Tracking

HOW TO ENTER A DOG SHOW

To enter a dog show in Britain, you need to look at one of the two dog papers, which come out on Fridays and can be ordered at any newsagent. Find the phone number of the secretary of a show, and call to obtain a timetable and entry form. Fill in the form with the classes you wish to enter (double-check your form!) and do not forget to send a cheque for the entries. Show entries close six weeks or so before the show.

You cannot enter the show if your dog is not registered with The Kennel Club. If you have sent off the forms to The Kennel Club to transfer the dog into your name, it is possible to enter with 'TAF' (transfer applied for) after the dog's name.

Dog (TD) and Patrol Dog (PD). As in conformation shows, dogs compete against a standard and, if the dog reaches the qualifying mark, it obtains a certificate. The exercises are divided into groups, and the dog must achieve at least 70% of the allotted score for each exercise in order to qualify. If the dog achieves 80% in the Open level, it receives a Certificate of Merit (COM); in the Champion-

CLASSES AT DOG SHOWS

There can be as many as 18 classes per sex for a breed, depending on its popularity. The classes offered can include Minor Puppy (ages 6 to 9 months), Puppy (ages 6 to 12 months), Junior (ages 6 to 18 months) and Beginners (handler or dog never won first place), as well as the following: Maiden; Novice; Tyro; Debutant; Undergraduate; Graduate; Postgraduate; Minor Limit; Mid Limit; Limit; Open; Veteran; Stud Dog; Brood Bitch; Progeny; Brace and Team. The schedule for the show, which comes with the entry form, explains each of the classes in detail.

COMPETITIVE FIELD WORK

In fieldwork, events may be competitively judged (the dog's performance is ranked against that of other dogs) or are non-competitive (the dog's performance is judged against a standard rather than ranked against that of another dog). For example, in the US, Sussex Spaniels are ineligible for interbreed competition such as field trials but are eligible to run with other spaniel breeds to attain criterion-based hunt titles. In the UK, Sussex Spaniels have a longer history of working in the field, actually competing successfully in trials before World War II, and have truly begun to hold their own in fieldwork when competing against other rare spaniel breeds such as the Welsh Springer Spaniel and Clumber Spaniel.

ship level, it receives a Qualifying Certificate.

At the CD stake, dogs must participate in four groups: Control, Stay, Agility and Search (Retrieve and Nosework). At the next three levels, UD, WD and TD, there are only three groups: Control, Agility and Nosework. The Agility exercises consist of three jumps: a vertical scale up a wall of planks; a clear jump over a basic hurdle with a removable top bar; and a long jump across angled planks.

To earn the UD, WD and TD,

dogs must track approximately one-half mile for articles laid from one-half hour to three hours previously. Tracks consist of turns and legs, and fresh ground is used for each participant. The fifth stake, PD, involves teaching manwork, which is not recommended for every breed.

AGILITY TRIALS

Agility trials began in the United Kingdom in 1977 and have since spread around the world, especially to the United States, where they are very popular. In fact, Sussex Spaniels have demonstrated superior ability in competitive agility in the United States, but have not been seen much in agility in other countries.

The handler directs his dog over an obstacle course that includes jumps (such as those used in the working trials), as well as tyres, the dog walk, weave poles, pipe tunnels, collapsed

tunnels, etc. The Kennel Club requires that dogs not be trained for agility until they are 12 months old, and the Sussex should be introduced and trained to jumping with extreme care. This dog sport is great fun for dog and owner, and interested owners should join a training club that has obstacles and experienced agility handlers who can introduce you and your dog to the 'ropes' (and tyres, tunnels, etc.).

The FCI governs most shows on the Continent. This photo was taken at a show in the Netherlands.

FÉDÉRATION CYNOLOGIQUE INTERNATIONALE

Established in 1911, the Fédération Cynologique Internationale (FCI) represents the 'world kennel

TALENTED TRACKER

An area of the dog sport for which the Sussex Spaniel is ideally suited is tracking. This sport that comes naturally and the Sussex excels in using his superior nose. Contact a Sussex Spaniel club for information on how you can become involved in tracking events, whether for competition or just for fun, with your Sussex.

The judge examines each dog physically to ensure the presence of correct bone structure and bite, traits that cannot be sufficiently evaluated simply by looking at the dog.

club.' This international body brings uniformity to the breeding, judging and showing of pure-bred dogs. Although the FCI originally included only five European nations: France, Germany, Austria, the Netherlands and Belgium (which remains its headquarters), the organisation today embraces nations on six continents and recognises well over 300 breeds of pure-bred dog.

The FCI sponsors both national and international shows. The hosting country determines the judging system and breed standards are always based on the breed's country of origin. Dogs from every country can participate in these impressive canine spectacles, the largest of which is the

World Dog Show, hosted in a different country each year.

There are three titles attainable through the FCI: the International Champion, which is the most prestigious; the International Beauty Champion, which is based on aptitude certificates in different countries; and the International Trial Champion, which is based on achievement in obedience trials in different countries.

The top award in an FCI show is the CAC (*Certificat d'Aptitude au Championnat*) and to gain a championship, a dog must win three CACs at regional or club shows under three different judges who are breed specialists. The title of International Champion is gained by winning four CACIBs (*Certificats d'Aptitude au Championnat International de Beauté*), which are offered only at international shows, with at least a one-year lapse between the first and fourth award.

COLOUR CONFUSION
The first-prize winner in Britain collects a red rosette and prize card. In the United States, red goes to the second-place winner, and it is the blue rosette that is awarded to the class winner. This difference in colours has led to some embarrassing situations when some have judged away from home!

FCI INFORMATION

There are 330 breeds recognised by the FCI, and each breed is considered to be 'owned' by a specific country. Each breed standard is a cooperative effort between the breed's country and the FCI's Standards and Scientific Commissions. Judges use these official breed standards at shows held in FCI member countries. One of the functions of the FCI is to update and translate the breed standards into French, English, Spanish and German.

The FCI is divided into ten groups and the Sussex Spaniel competes in Group 8 for Retrievers, Flushing dogs and Water dogs. At the World Dog Show, the following classes are offered for each breed: Puppy Class (6–9 months), Junior Class (9–18 months), Open Class (15 months or older) and Champion Class. A dog can be awarded a classification of Excellent, Very Good, Good, Sufficient and Not Sufficient. Puppies can be awarded classifications of Very Promising, Promising or Not Promising. Four placements are made in each class. After all classes are judged, a Best of Breed is selected. Other special groups and classes may also be shown. Each exhibitor showing a dog receives a written evaluation from the judge.

Besides the World Dog Show and other all-breed shows, you can exhibit your dog at speciality shows held by different breed clubs. Speciality shows may have their own regulations.

DID YOU KNOW?

The FCI *does not* issue pedigrees. The FCI members and contract partners are responsible for issuing pedigrees and training judges in their own countries. The FCI does maintain a list of judges and makes sure that they are recognised throughout the FCI member countries.

The FCI also *does not* act as a breeder referral; breeder information is available from FCI-recognised national canine societies in each of the FCI's member countries.

A treat in the ring gets the dog to stand at attention and look his best.

BEHAVIOUR OF YOUR
SUSSEX SPANIEL

As a Sussex Spaniel owner, you have selected your dog so that you and your loved ones can have a companion, a hunter, a friend and a four-legged family member. You invest time, money and effort to care for and train the family's new charge. Of course, this chosen canine behaves perfectly! Well, perfectly like a *dog*.

THINK LIKE A DOG
Dogs do not think like humans, nor do humans think like dogs, though we try. Unfortunately, a dog is incapable of comprehending how humans think, so the responsibility falls on the owner to adopt a proper canine mindset. Dogs cannot rationalise, and dogs exist in the present moment. Many dog owners make the mistake in training of thinking that they can reprimand their dog for something he did a while ago. Basically, you cannot even reprimand a dog for something he did 20 seconds ago! Either catch him in the act or forget it! It is a waste of your and your dog's time—in his mind, you are reprimanding him for whatever he is doing at that moment.

The following behavioural problems represent some which owners most commonly encounter. Every dog is unique and every situation is unique. No author could purport for you to solve your Sussex Spaniel's problems simply by reading a script. Here we outline some basic 'dogspeak' so that owners' chances of solving behavioural problems are increased.

Discuss bad habits with your veterinary surgeon and he can recommend a behavioural specialist to consult in appropriate cases. Since behavioural abnormalities are the main reason for owners' abandoning their pets, we hope that you will make a valiant effort to solve your Sussex Spaniel's problems. Patience and understanding are virtues that must dwell in every pet-loving household.

SEPARATION ANXIETY
Sussex Spaniels can be intensely involved in the daily lives of their human pack. They are not a 'go lie down and leave me alone' kind of dog. Sussex Spaniels actively seek human companionship and

generally will work hard to get it. The breed must have significant daily human interaction to be at its best.

This being said, separation anxiety is recognised by behaviourists as the most common form of stress for dogs, and it can also lead to destructive behaviours. It's more than your Sussex Spaniel's howling his displeasure at your leaving the house and his being left alone. This is a normal reaction, no different from the child who cries as his mother leaves him on the first day at school. However, separation anxiety is more serious.

Obviously, you enjoy spending time with your dog, and he thrives on your love and attention. However, it should not become a dependent relationship in which he is heartbroken without you. This broken heart can also bring on destructive behaviour as well as loss of appetite, depression and lack of interest in play and interaction. Canine behaviourists have been spending much time and energy to help owners better understand the significance of this stressful condition.

One thing you can do to minimise separation anxiety is to make your entrances and exits as low-key as possible. Do not give your dog a long drawn-out goodbye, and do not lavish him with hugs and kisses when you return. This is giving in to the attention that he craves, and it will only make him miss it more when you are away. Another thing you can try is to give your dog a treat when you leave; this will not only keep him occupied and keep his mind off the fact that you have just left but it will also help him associate your leaving with a pleasant experience.

You may have to accustom your dog to being left alone at

AGE OF ANXIETY

The number of dogs that suffer from separation anxiety is on the rise as more and more pet owners find themselves at work all day. New attention is being paid to this problem, which is especially hard to diagnose since it is only evident when the dog is alone. Research is currently being done to help educate dog owners about separation anxiety and how they can help minimise this problem in their dogs.

PHARMACEUTICAL FIX

There are two drugs specifically designed to treat mental problems in dogs. About 7 million dogs each year are destroyed because owners can no longer tolerate their dogs' behaviour, according to Nicholas Dodman, a specialist in animal behaviour at Tufts University in Massachusetts.

The first drug, Clomicalm, is prescribed for dogs suffering from separation anxiety, which is said to cause them to react when left alone by barking, chewing their owners' belongings, drooling copiously or defecating or urinating inside the home.

The second drug, Anipryl, is recommended for cognitive dysfunction syndrome or 'old-dog syndrome,' a mental deterioration that comes with age. Such dogs often seem to forget that they were house-trained and where their food bowls are, and they may even fail to recognise their owners.

A tremendous human-animal bonding relationship is established with all dogs, particularly veteran dogs. This precious relationship deteriorates when the dog does not recognise his master. The drug can restore the bond and make veteran dogs feel more like their old selves.

intervals. Of course, when your dog starts whimpering as you approach the door, your first instinct will be to run to him and comfort him, but do not do it! Really—eventually he will adjust to your absence. His anxiety stems from being placed in an unfamiliar situation; by familiarising him with being alone, he will learn that he will survive. That is not to say you should purposely leave your dog home alone, but the dog needs to know that, while he can depend on you for his care, you do not have to be by his side 24 hours a day. Some behaviourists recommend tiring the dog out before you leave home—take him for a good long walk or engage in a game of fetch in the garden.

When the dog is alone in the house, he should be placed in his crate—another distinct advantage to crate training your dog. The crate should be placed in his familiar happy family area, where

I'M HOME!

Dogs left alone for varying lengths of time may often react wildly when their owners return. Sometimes they run, jump, bite, chew, tear things apart, wet themselves, gobble their food or behave in other undisciplined ways. If your dog behaves in this manner upon your return home, allow him to calm down before greeting him or he will consider your attention as a reward for his antics.

he normally sleeps and already feels comfortable, thereby making him feel more at ease when he is alone. Be sure to give the dog a special chew toy to enjoy while he settles into his crate.

AGGRESSION

The Sussex Spaniel should not be an aggressive breed; in fact, the breed standard states that he should have a 'kindly disposition' and that aggression is 'highly undesirable.' Nonetheless, aggression is a problem that concerns all responsible dog owners since, when not controlled, aggression always becomes dangerous. An aggressive dog, no matter the size, may lunge at, bite or even attack a person or another dog.

Aggressive behaviour is not to be tolerated. It is more than just inappropriate behaviour; it is painful for a family to watch their dog become unpredictable in his behaviour to the point where they are afraid of him. While not all aggressive behaviour is dangerous, growling, baring teeth, etc. can be frightening. It is important to ascertain why the dog is acting in this manner. Aggression is a display of dominance, and the dog should not have the dominant role in his pack, which is, in this case, your family.

Sussex Spaniels are often possessive of their owners, which may be misinterpreted as aggression. A Sussex may live happily

with other dogs, provided they are trained and socialised to do so. However, the Sussex prefers to be the 'top dog' and care should be taken in introducing another dog to the household. Disputes can arise over 'possessions,' be it a favoured toy or even the owner himself. It cannot be said enough that early socialisation plays a large role in avoiding aggressive behaviour.

If a Sussex exhibits aggressive tendencies, behaviour modification techniques should be used. Interventions must rely on techniques that avoid overly corrective manoeuvres. It is just good sense that corrective measures that are physical in nature may be seen as aggressive by a dog of any breed. This increases the likelihood that the dog will respond aggressively. In this scenario, the aggression escalates.

It is important not to challenge an aggressive dog, as

The Sussex is loyal and affectionate, thriving on attention from his owner. Be sure to spend time with your Sussex if you are out of the house all day—let him know that he is a valued member of the family!

DOGS HAVE FEELINGS, TOO

You probably don't realise how much your dog notices the presence of a new person in your home as well as the loss of a familiar face. If someone new has moved in with you, your pet will need help adjusting. Have the person feed your dog or accompany the two of you on a walk. Also, make sure your roommate is aware of the rules and routines you have already set for your dog.

If you have just lost a longtime companion, there is a chance you could end up with a case of 'leave me, leave my dog.' Dogs experience separation anxiety and depression, so watch for any changes in sleeping and eating habits and try to lavish a little extra love on your dog. It might make you feel better, too.

this could provoke an attack. Observe your Sussex Spaniel's body language. Does he make direct eye contact and stare? Does he try to make himself as large as possible: ears pricked, chest out, tail erect? Height and size signify authority in a dog pack—being taller or 'above' another dog literally means that he is 'above' in social status. These body signals tell you that your Sussex Spaniel thinks he is in charge, a problem that needs to be addressed. An aggressive dog is

unpredictable; you never know when he is going to strike and what he is going to do. You cannot understand why a dog that is playful one minute is growling the next.

Fear is a common cause of aggression in dogs. Perhaps your Sussex Spaniel had a negative experience as a puppy, which causes him to be fearful when a similar situation presents itself later in life. The dog may act aggressively in order to protect himself from whatever is making him afraid. It is not always easy to determine what is making your dog fearful, but if you can isolate what brings out the fear reaction, you can help the dog overcome it.

Supervise your Sussex Spaniel's interactions with people and other dogs, and praise the dog when it goes well. If he starts to act aggressively in a situation, correct him and remove him from the situation. Do not let people approach the dog and start petting him without your express permission. That way, you can have the

DOMINANT AGGRESSION

Never allow your puppy to growl at you or bare his tiny teeth. Such behaviour is dominant and aggressive. If not corrected, the dog will repeat the behaviour, which will become more threatening as he grows larger and will eventually lead to biting.

dog sit to accept petting, and praise him when he behaves properly. You are focusing on praise and on modifying his behaviour by rewarding him when he acts appropriately. By being gentle and by supervising his interactions, you are showing him that there is no need to be afraid or defensive.

The best solution is to consult a behavioural specialist, one who has experience with the breed, or at least with spaniels. Together,

BE NOT AFRAID
Just like humans, dogs can suffer from phobias including fear of thunder, fear of heights, fear of stairs or even fear of specific objects such as the swimming pool. To help your dog overcome his fear, first determine what is causing the phobia. For example, your dog may be generalising by associating an accident that occurred on one set of stairs with every step he sees. You can try desensitisation training, which involves introducing the fear-trigger to your dog slowly, in a relaxed setting, and rewarding him when he remains calm. Most importantly, when your dog responds fearfully, do not coddle or try to soothe him, as this only makes him think that his fear is okay.

perhaps you can pinpoint the cause of your dog's aggression and do something about it. An aggressive dog cannot be trusted, and a dog that cannot be trusted is not safe to have as a family pet. If, very unusually, you find that your pet has become untrustworthy and you feel it necessary to seek a new home with a more suitable family and environment, explain fully to the new owners all your reasons for rehoming the dog to be fair to all concerned. Though it is doubtful that aggression would progress to such a level in the Sussex, in the very worst case, you will have to consider euthanasia.

SEXUAL BEHAVIOUR
Dogs exhibit certain sexual behaviours that may have influenced your choice of male or female when you first purchased your Sussex Spaniel. To a certain extent, spaying/neutering will eliminate these behaviours, but if

Sussex Spaniels should be non-aggressive by nature, including toward other dogs, although this needs to be nurtured by careful introduction and socialisation.

FEAR IN A GROWN DOG

Fear in a grown dog is often the result of improper or incomplete socialisation as a pup, or it can be the result of a traumatic experience he suffered when young. Keep in mind that the term 'traumatic' is relative—something that you would not think twice about can leave a lasting negative impression on a puppy. If the dog experiences a similar experience later in life, he may try to fight back to protect himself. Again, this behaviour is very unpredictable, especially if you do not know what is triggering his fear.

you are purchasing a dog that you wish to breed from, you should be aware of what you will have to deal with throughout the dog's life.

Female dogs usually have two oestruses per year, with each season lasting about three weeks. These are the only times in which a female dog will mate, and she usually will not allow this until the second week of the cycle, although this varies from bitch to bitch. If not bred during the heat cycle, it is not uncommon for a bitch to experience a false pregnancy, in which her mammary glands swell and she exhibits maternal tendencies toward toys or other objects.

With male dogs, owners must be aware that whole dogs (dogs who are not neutered) have the natural inclination to mark their territory. Males mark their territory by spraying small amounts of urine as they lift their legs in a macho ritual. Marking can occur both outdoors in the garden and around the neighbourhood as well as indoors on furniture legs, curtains and the sofa. Such behaviour can be very frustrating for the owner; early training is strongly urged before the 'urge' strikes your dog. Neutering the male at an appropriate early age can solve this problem before it becomes an habit.

Other problems associated with males are wandering and mounting. Both of these habits, of course, belong to the unneutered dog, whose sexual drive leads him away from home in search of the bitch in heat. Males will mount females in heat, as well as any other dog, male or female, that happens to catch their fancy.

NO BUTTS ABOUT IT

Dogs get to know each other by sniffing each other's backsides. It seems that each dog has a telltale odour, probably created by the anal glands. It also distinguishes sex and signals when a female will be receptive to a male's attention. Some dogs snap at another dog's intrusion of their private parts.

Other possible mounting partners include his owner, the furniture, guests to the home and friends you meet on the street. Discourage such behaviour early on.

Owners must further recognise that mounting is not merely a sexual expression but also one of dominance. Be consistent and be persistent, and you will find that you can 'move mounters.'

BARKING

Dogs cannot talk—oh, what they would say if they could! Instead, barking is a dog's way of 'talking.' It can be somewhat frustrating

because it is not always easy to tell what a dog means by his bark—is he excited, happy, frightened or angry? Whatever it is that the dog is trying to say, he should not be punished for barking. It is only when the barking becomes excessive, and when the excessive barking becomes a bad habit, that the behaviour needs to be modified.

Some Sussex Spaniels are quite vocal, using their barks to alert owners of suspicious noises and such. Many Sussex Spaniels express their enthusiasm for an activity, such as being released from a crate for training and work, with brief, happy barks or yips. They are also vocally responsive to their owners, who elicit the comical Sussex snort and barking as part of play and other interac-

---

QUIET ON THE SET

To encourage proper barking, you can teach your dog the command 'quiet.' When someone comes to the door and the dog barks a few times, praise him. Talk to him soothingly and, when he stops barking, tell him 'Quiet' and continue to praise him. In this sense you are letting him bark his warning, which is an instinctive behaviour, and then rewarding him for being quiet after a few barks. You may initially reward him with a treat after he has been quiet for a few minutes.

MACHO GUSTO

Males, whether castrated or not, will mount almost anything: a pillow, your leg or, much to your horror, even your neighbour's leg. As with other types of inappropriate behaviour, the dog must be corrected while in the act, which for once is not difficult. Often he will not let go! While a puppy is experimenting with his very first urges, his owners feel he needs to 'sow his oats' and allow the pup to mount. As the pup grows into a full-size dog, with full-size urges, it becomes a nuisance and an embarrassment. Males always appear as if they are trying to 'save the race,' more determined and stronger than imaginable. While altering the dog at an appropriate age will limit the dog's desire, it usually does not remove it entirely.

tions. The Sussex's vocalisations are expressive and range from yips and yodels to barks and howls. Fanciers report that an household with more than one Sussex may have a vocal chorus, as howling in unison is not unknown.

The Sussex Spaniel's vocalisations are a unique trait of the breed and should not be discouraged unless they become habitual and excessive. This is a problem that should be corrected early on. Sussex Spaniels must be taught when it is appropriate to use their expressive voices; teaching a 'quiet' command is highly recommended.

As your Sussex Spaniel grows up, you will be able to tell when his barking is purposeful and when it is for no reason. You will become able to distinguish your dog's different barks and their meanings. For example, the bark when someone comes to the door will be different from the bark when he is excited to see you. It is similar to a person's tone of voice, except that the dog has to rely totally on tone of voice because he does not have the benefit of using words. An incessant barker will be evident at an early age.

There are some things that encourage a dog to bark. For example, if your dog barks non-stop for a few minutes and you give him a treat to quieten him, he believes that you are rewarding him for barking. He will associate barking with getting a treat and will keep doing it until he is rewarded. On the other hand, if you give him a command such as 'Quiet' and praise him after he has stopped barking for a few seconds, he will get the idea that being 'quiet' is what you want him to do.

DIGGING

Digging, which is seen as a destructive behaviour to humans, is actually quite a natural behaviour in dogs. Although terriers (the 'earth dogs') are most associated with the digging, any dog's desire to dig can be irrepressible and most frustrating to his owners. When digging occurs in your garden, it is actually a normal behaviour redirected into something the dog

HE'S PROTECTING YOU

Barking is your dog's way of protecting you. If he barks at a stranger walking past your house, a moving car or a fleeing cat, he is merely exercising his responsibility to protect his pack (YOU) and territory from a perceived intruder.

Since the 'intruder' usually keeps going, the dog thinks his barking chased it away and he feels fulfilled. This behaviour leads your overly vocal friend to believe that he is the 'dog in charge.'

can do in his everyday life. In the wild, a dog would be actively seeking food, making his own shelter, etc. He would be using his paws in a purposeful manner for his survival. Since you provide him with food and shelter, he has no need to use his paws for these purposes, and so the energy that he would be using may manifest itself in the form of little holes all over your garden and flower beds.

Sussex Spaniels are notorious problem solvers, which means that they may turn their digging talents into 'solving the problem' of confinement in the fenced garden. For this reason, fences must be embedded securely into the ground at a depth of at least one foot, and fences must be kept in good repair. Inspect the fence regularly to check for evidence of an escape artist at work, and secure any gaps or holes.

Perhaps your Sussex is digging as a reaction to boredom—it is somewhat similar to someone eating a whole bag of crisps in front of the TV—because they are there and there is nothing better to do! Basically, the answer is to provide the dog with adequate play and exercise so that his mind and paws are occupied, and so that he feels as if he is doing something useful.

Of course, digging is easiest to control if it is stopped as soon as possible, but it is often hard to catch a dog in the act. If your dog

NO KISSES
We all love our dogs and our dogs love us. They show their love and affection by licking us. This is not a very sanitary practice, as dogs lick and sniff in some unsavoury places. Kissing your dog on the mouth is strictly forbidden, as parasites can be transmitted in this manner.

is a compulsive digger and is not easily distracted by other activities, you can designate an area on your property where he is allowed to dig. If you catch him digging in an off-limits area of the garden, immediately bring him to the approved area and praise him for digging there. Keep a close eye on him so that you can catch him in the act—that is the only way to make him understand what is permitted and what is not. If you take him to an hole he dug an

Digging is a natural instinct for most dogs, though you may not appreciate your Sussex's gardening talents. While difficult to stop entirely, digging behaviour can be modified and controlled.

hour ago and tell him 'No,' he will understand that you are not fond of holes, or dirt or flowers. If you catch him while he is stifle-deep in your tulips, that is when he will get your message.

CHEWING

The national canine pastime is chewing! Every dog loves to sink his 'canines' into a tasty bone but, if a bone is not readily available, he'll gladly sink his teeth into whatever he can find. Dogs need to chew, to massage their gums, to

make their new teeth feel better and to exercise their jaws. This is a natural behaviour that is deeply embedded in all things canine. Our role as owners is not to stop the dog's chewing, but rather to redirect it to positive, chew-worthy objects.

Sussex Spaniels are known to resort to chewing to entertain themselves if bored. Be an informed owner and purchase proper chew toys, like strong nylon bones, that will not splinter. Be sure that the objects are safe and durable, since your dog's safety is at risk. Again, the owner is responsible for ensuring a dog-proof environment. Items like rawhide, chew hooves and the like are not recommended. They can become messy and destroyed in no time, and have been known to result in digestive ailments, sometimes requiring surgery.

Along with providing safe, proper chew devices, prevention is the key; that is, put your shoes, handbags and other tasty objects in their proper places (out of the reach of the growing canine mouth). Direct puppies to their toys whenever you see them 'tasting' the furniture legs or the leg of your trousers. Make a loud noise to attract the pup's attention and immediately escort him to his chew toy and engage him with the toy for at least four minutes, praising and encouraging him all the while. An array of safe,

SMILE!
Dogs and humans may be the only animals that smile. A dog will imitate the smile on his owner's face when he greets a friend. The dog only smiles at his human friends; he never smiles at another dog or cat. Usually, a dog rolls up his lips and shows his teeth in a clenched mouth while rolling over onto his back, begging for a soft scratch.

interesting chew toys will keep your dog's mind and teeth occupied, and distracted from chewing on things he shouldn't.

Some trainers recommend deterrents, such as hot pepper, a bitter spice or a product designed for this purpose, to discourage the dog from chewing unwanted objects. Test these products to see which works best before investing in large quantities.

JUMPING UP
Jumping up is a dog's friendly way of saying hello! Some dog owners do not mind when their dog jumps up. The problem arises when guests come to the house and the dog greets them in the same manner—whether they like it or not! However friendly the greeting may be, the chances are that your visitors will not appreciate your dog's enthusiasm. The dog will not be able to distinguish upon whom he can jump and whom he cannot. Therefore, it is probably best to discourage this behaviour entirely.

Pick a command such as 'Off' (avoid using 'Down' since you will use that for the dog to lie down) and tell him 'Off' when he jumps up. Place him on the ground on all fours and have him sit, praising him the whole time. Always lavish him with praise and petting when he is in the sit position. In this way, you can give him a warm affectionate greeting, let him know that you are as glad to see him as he is to see you and instil good manners at the same time!

FOOD STEALING

Is your dog devising ways of stealing food from your coffee table or kitchen counter? If so, you must answer the following questions: Is your Sussex Spaniel peckish, or is he 'constantly famished' like many dogs seem to be? Face it, some dogs are more food-motivated than others. They are totally obsessed by the smell of food and can only think of their next meal. Food stealing is terrific fun and always yields a great reward—FOOD, glorious food.

Your goal as an owner, therefore, is to be sensible about where food is placed in the home and to reprimand your dog whenever he is caught in the act of stealing. But remember, only reprimand your dog if you actually see him stealing, not later when the crime is discovered; that will be of no use at all and will only serve to confuse him.

BEGGING

Just like food stealing, begging is a favourite pastime of peckish puppies! It achieves that same lovely result—FOOD! Dogs quickly learn that their owners keep the 'good food' for themselves, and that we humans do not dine on dried food alone. Begging is a conditioned response

A well-trained and well-behaved Sussex knows that his attention should be on something other than his owner's lunch.

related to a specific stimulus, time and place. The sounds of the kitchen, cans and bottles opening, crinkling bags, the smell of food in preparation, etc., will excite the dog, and soon the paws will be in the air!

Here is the solution to stopping this behaviour: Never give in to a beggar! You are rewarding the dog for sitting pretty, jumping up, whining and rubbing his nose into you by giving him food. By ignoring the dog, you will (eventually) force the behaviour into extinction. Note that the behaviour is likely to get worse before it disappears, so be sure there are not any 'softies' in the family who will give in to little 'Oliver' every time he whimpers, 'More, please.'

COPROPHAGIA

Faeces eating is, to humans, one of the most disgusting behaviours that their dogs could engage in, yet, to dogs, it is perfectly normal. It is hard for us to understand why a dog would want to eat his own faeces. He could be seeking certain nutrients that are missing from his diet, he could be just plain hungry or he could be attracted by the pleasing (to a dog) scent. While coprophagia most often refers to the dog's eating his own faeces, a dog may just as likely eat that of another animal as well if he comes across it. Dogs often find the stool of cats and

horses more palatable than that of other dogs.

Vets have found that diets with low levels of digestibility, containing relatively low levels of fibre and high levels of starch, increase coprophagia. Therefore, high-fibre diets may decrease the likelihood of dogs' eating faeces. Both the consistency of the stool (how firm it feels in the dog's mouth) and the presence of undigested nutrients increase the likelihood. Once the dog develops diarrhoea from faeces eating, he will likely stop this distasteful habit.

To discourage this behaviour, first make sure that the food you are feeding your dog is nutrition- ally complete and that he is getting enough food. If changes in his diet do not seem to work, and no medical cause can be found, you will have to modify the behaviour through environmental control before it becomes an habit. The best way to prevent your dog from eating his stool is to make it unavailable—clean up after he eliminates and remove any stool from the garden. If it is not there, he cannot eat it.

Reprimanding for stool eating rarely impresses the dog. Vets recommend distracting the dog while he is in the act of stool eating. Coprophagia is seen most frequently in pups 6 to 12 months of age, and usually disappears around the dog's first birthday.

INDEX

My Sussex Spaniel

PUT YOUR PUPPY'S FIRST PICTURE HERE

Dog's Name _____

Date _____ Photographer _____